Introduction to Structured Water with Clayton Nolte

Overview of the Health Benefits, Cost Savings and Environmental Advantages of Structured Water

Compiled by Charles Betterton

Concept and Formatting by Charles Betterton
Based on Interviews with and Articles by Inventor Clayton Nolte

Published by Ultimate Destiny Network, Inc.
PO Box 20072, Sedona, AZ 86341
www.UltimateStructuredWater.info

Version 1.0. March 2011

Limits of Liability and Disclaimer of Warranty

The author and publisher of this book and the associated materials have used their best efforts in preparing this material. The author and publisher make no representations or warranties with respect to the accuracy, applicability, fitness, or completeness of the contents of this material.

They disclaim any warranties expressed or implied, merchantability, or fitness for any particular purpose. The author and publisher shall in no event be held liable for any loss or other damages, including but not limited to special, incidental, consequential, or other damages.

If you have any doubts about anything, the advice of a competent professional should be sought. This material contains elements protected under International and Federal Copyright laws and treaties. Any unauthorized reprint or use of this material is prohibited.

Disclaimer:

None of the statements on any page of this publication have been submitted for review, nor have they been approved by the FDA or any other regulatory agency. This publication is intended to provide educational information about our products and nothing stated is intended as medical advice or counseling. Please contact your doctor or medical practitioner with any questions about any health matter or condition.

Table of Contents

About Clayton Nolte

Clayton M. Nolte worked for forty years in the military and as a consultant in Research and Development. Clayton's assignments included developing new technologies that emulate nature and reengineering existing electronic devices for easy operation in the modern era.

During Clayton's research, nature's own structured water became a unique recurring phenomenon in his life, often appearing where no water should. With an innate desire to produce such water for more in-depth studies in remote locations and labs, Clayton delved into the inner World of water.

Since that time, Clayton has discovered innovative technologies, fabricated several structured water devices and proved the science. His life experience is in infinite possibilities. Drawing on that experience, he is forming an alliance of discovery that will together cross the bridge into the new paradigm for the future of water.

Inventor Clayton Nolte with the Natural Action Structured Water Devices.

To contact Clayton or submit a question for him to answer, please visit our blog site page at http://ultimatewater.wordpress.com/clayton-nolte/

Introduction to Structured Water

> **"When we understand that our innate life blood and Structured Water are one and the same—and both are the truth of Nature -- we then know we are standing in the doorway to fulfill our Destiny. We are in the Grace of Receivership."-- Clayton Nolte, inventor of Natural Action Structured Water Devices**

"The air, the water and the ground are free gifts to man and no one has the power to portion them out in parcels. Man must drink and breathe and walk and therefore each man has a right to his share of each."

– James Fennimore Cooper (1789-1851), The Prairie 1827

Seventy-five percent of North Americans are chronically dehydrated. Even mild dehydration slows metabolism, causes fatigue, reduces short-term memory, and increases existing health challenges. Drinking the more water is important, but drinking the *right* water is even more important.

Water is one of the most essential components of the human body. It regulates the body's temperature, cushions and protects vital organs, and aids the digestive system. It creates an infinitely malleable volume that literally allows movement to be possible. Without water, our bodies would be like stone.

Water not only composes 75 % of all muscle tissue and about 10% of fatty tissue, it exists both inside and outside every cell. Within the cells, water transports nutrients and dispels waste. It is impossible to sustain human life for more than a week without water. It is also impossible to be healthy if water's life-giving properties are not optimal.

Structured Water is optimal water. Drinking it is the most fundamental way to help the body function optimally and remain disease-free. Structured water is hydrating water. Drinking Structured Water throughout each day assists the body's ability to be energized via delivery of hydrogen "fuel" (hence, the term *hydration*), and enables the body to flush toxins and metabolic waste.

Research has shown that proper hydration may minimize chronic pains such as rheumatoid arthritis, lower back pain, and colitis, as well as lower cholesterol and blood pressure. Most health practitioners advise that, if we simply drank enough water to keep our bodies sufficiently hydrated, many of the chronic diseases from which we suffer today would be abated.

Research also has shown chronic dehydration to be the root cause of many diseases associated with aging, including arthritis, GI disorders, and senile dementia. To complicate the situation, natural thirst signals decline as we become accustomed to being dehydrated over the years. Dehydration in the elderly is a real, but *correctable,* problem.

When it comes to hydration, all water is *not* equal. Structured Water releases stable oxygen. It delivers this oxygen to a greater degree than ordinary water; in fact, ordinary water may require the body to *take* resources from other areas in order to process the water.

Our bodies contain structured water when we are born. However, as the body grows older and is subjected to stress, contamination, pollutants, free radicals, poor diet and other external factors, the body begins to dehydrate. The structured cell water with which we are born diminishes, and the cell loses its effective shape. The result is that our ability to absorb water decreases as we age.

When you use a Structured Water Unit, you can actually smell, feel, and taste the difference immediately. Think of what proper hydration might mean to your family's good health and well-being.

Using a Structured Water unit means you can drink water directly from your tap. Think of how that translates into savings: you are spared the expense of having to buy bottled water, and the environment is spared all those discarded plastic water bottles.

Structured Water also tastes pure, smooth and clean. Some people state it has a sweeter taste than other waters.

Structured Water Oxygen

Structured Water contains stable oxygen, which does not dissipate immediately. This added oxygen can help to raise the oxygen content in the blood by up to 10 points on a 100-point scale. Low oxygen content in the blood has been associated with poor health and headaches.

Structured Water is great for high altitudes where oxygen concentration is lower.

How important is oxygen?

90% of all "life energy" is created by oxygen.

All functions in the body are regulated by oxygen.

The brain processes billions of bits of information per second—thanks to oxygen.

Structured Water is Much More Than Just Water!

Research has demonstrated that Structured Water:

▶ Helps increase or improve Hydration on an intra- and extra–cellular level in 22 minutes.

▶ Helps detoxify the cells through superior hydration.

▶ Helps balance pH by establishing more alkalinity.

▶ Helps double the immune system response in only 7 days.

▶ Helps reduce blood pressure.

▶ Helps increase Oxygen content in the blood (helps alleviate altitude sickness).

▶ Helps increase thought processing, mental awareness and creativity.

▶ Helps reduce swollen joints that are associated with arthritis.

▶ Helps establish better health and overall vitality.

Bio-Photon Energy

The Natural Action Structured Water Unit Truly is Amazing Technology

The Natural Action Structured Water Units incorporate technology that applies an advanced understanding of vortex science, utilizing the dynamic characteristic of water and geometric structures that allow the water to work upon itself on the molecular level to create naturally balanced water. Water is the machine. There are no moving parts or chemicals. The process is totally pure—just like water coursing along in a beautiful river.

"Ultimate Water" is created at the molecular level when some force alters the basic molecular structure of the water. Structured water is water in which the healthful benefits of minerals and other positive characteristics have been activated and retained. At the same time, excess suspended solids, including contaminants and sediment, are dynamically isolated or removed.

A specially tuned geometry creates an energy environment in which the water can structure itself. This geometric technology breaks up large, low-energy water molecule clusters into smaller, high-energy clusters. Structuring gives water a lower surface tension and better hydrating properties.

The systematic treatment of water eliminates negative energy patterns (sometimes called the "memory" of water) and redefines the water's natural, healthy energy pattern. Structured water allows us to imprint, through our DNA and RNA, the knowledge of its secret blue- print. With this information, we become more balanced in the universe.

Structured water fights toxins such as chlorine, fluoride, and anaerobic bacteria—straight from your shower and tap.

Structured water can be called "empowered water" because its molecules hold an excess stable oxygen. This oxygen helps the body assimilate this water to a much greater degree than ordinary water. Our bodies contain structured water when we are born.

However, as the human body grows older, it is subjected to stress, contamination, pollutants, free radicals, poor diet, and other external factors. The body begins to dehydrate, and the structured cell water with which we were born begins to diminish, losing its effective shape.

The result is that our ability to absorb water begins to decrease as we age. The following photos are water molecules frozen and viewed under a 20,000x microscope.

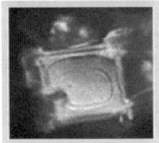 **Empowered Oxygenated water is readily accepted by the body and helps energize the body.**

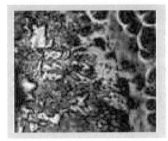 **Distilled or Reverse Osmosis waters pull electrolytes and minerals out of the body and they carry very little free oxygen.**

 **Tap water is "dead" water and cannot be fully utilized by the body.**

The Process of Structuring Water

The process by which structured water is created may seem bewildering, because the technology uses no moving parts or electricity, requires no maintenance, and is offered with a lifetime warranty. The concept is hard for some to grasp, because it seems so simple.

So ask yourself, what does nature do to water? Water in nature is almost never still; the rivers flow, oceans surge, and even lakes are continually undergoing evaporation/condensation. Natural water is active.

To structure water, it must be put into motion. The structuring process uses the motion of the flowing water as the source of energy to drive the device. In the structuring chamber, the water is moved against specifically placed geometric forms that cause the water to swirl and vortex to it maximum potential.

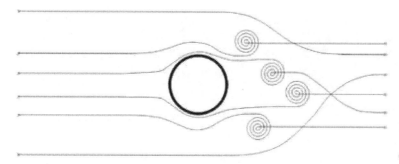

Clustering

Clustering: All water is clustered, meaning that water is made up of clusters of gathered molecules. Most tap and bottled waters are in clusters of 80– 100+ molecules per cluster. The cluster is held together internally by electromagnetic bonds; other elements in the water, such as calcium, sodium, and pollutants, are also magnetically attracted to these clusters.

As the large water clusters move against the geometric forms, they are caused to spin; the centrifugal force and multi-directional spinning breaks the clusters into smaller clusters of 5- 20 molecules each. This happens when the electromagnetic bonding within the water clusters becomes overpowered by the energy of the centrifugal force of the spinning cluster.

In this state, the water is only able to connect with itself, making each individual cluster pure and perfect. The minerals found in water that is in this state are neutral, meaning that they cannot attach themselves to anything in their path. This allows them to pass through our elimination system with ease.

Surface Tension and Drinking the Right Water

Source:	Dynes/cubic centimetre
Distilled/City waters	72-78
Most bottled water	72
Cellular membrane	46
Nature Hydration Structured Water	43
Alcohol	28

A human being is a walking mass of more than one trillion cells. If we are drinking water that is not able to hydrate our cells, can we stay properly hydrated? In most cases, we do not. That is why the question of how much water we drink is not as important as what *kind* of water we are drinking.

Water does us no good if our cells cannot benefit from it. Many of us are victims of chronic dehydration because we think we are properly hydrating ourselves. If we have symptoms of dehydration, but think we're drinking enough water, we might start to look elsewhere for the cause our condition.

Communicating With Water by Clayton Nolte

Here's something you may want to express to the universe (God) when you are in the space of wanting to change your life: Just before you are about to go to sleep, ask that all your demands, prayers and/or requests that have not been made manifest be erased.

You may have to see them on a big black board and physically erase them, or you may have to blow them up, but do not review them or bring them into mind; this just reinforces them to be more in your life. When you wake up, you will feel alive, awake, alert, and exuberant.

Another exercise is this: Before you go to bed at night, fill up a paper cup (a white, natural, recycled cup would be best) with the purest water you can find, preferably natural spring water (not distilled) from a verified pure source.

Before lying down, close your eyes, thank the universe for your day, and focus on what you would like your reality to be for tomorrow. What would you like the universe to bring to you or show you, and what would you like to give?

After you have in your mind what you would specifically like from the universe tomorrow, look at your paper cup of water and focus those thoughts unto the water as if the water were the whole universe (it is).

Then, to further manifest and have the water help you, write on the paper cup your wishes or intentions that you thought of for tomorrow. Sometimes this may just be a general good principal, such as, "tomorrow I would like to be amazingly creative and glowing with love," or it can be very specific, such as, "tomorrow I would like to solve my challenge with such and such a situation."

After you do this with complete clarity of mind and gratitude, drink half of the cup of water. Then go to sleep knowing that the water is reverberating with great intensity and acting as a magnifying antenna to the universe.

The water in your body that you drank already has your intentions in it and is still connected to the water in the cup, which is connected to EVERYTHING and is doing its best to help you send your message to the universe.

The water's structure IS actually changing to your thought, and this is provable by science to even the most skeptical naysayers. As you sleep, your subconscious mind will continue to communicate with the water—both the water in your body and that still in the cup—and it will change its structure into what you concentrated on.

When you wake up in the morning and drink the other half of the cup of water, you will literally be drinking your dreams!

This will make your intentions reverberate even more powerfully through your whole being. Do this every night, and see what happens. Miracles will multiply and health will improve at ever-faster rates. Water is the most beautiful, mutable, and thought-affected physical substance we humans have.

Water is the ultimate physical manifestation within the hologram of our existence. If you love your water, it will love you back and help you along your path. Water is alive and aware. **Be in joy!**

Clayton Nolte introducing Structured Water at an Ultimate Destiny University program with Will Tuttle (www.willtuttle.com) on his Book, *The World Peace Diet* at the Sedona Creative Life Center.

"When we all come together and we are all in joy and we are doing what we are meant to do, then it will be just like a river, we will be in the flow. You will sing my song: I'm alive, awake, alert, enthusiastic. This is how I choose to start my day. Alive, awake, alert. Alive, awake, alert. Alive, awake, alert, enthusiastic today. Make life absolutely perfect."

-- Clayton Nolte, inventor of Natural Action Structured Water Devices

Chapter 1. How is Water Structured?

(From an interview of Clayton Nolte by Wes Whittaker)

Water is meant to contain life force energy, and that life force energy is found within the water molecule itself. Each water molecule has the power, and the individual mandate, to protect life. Its job is to generously provide the things that are good for life and to protect against the things that are harmful. Water protects us by locking away the things that are adverse to life. Impurities are pulled to the inside of the molecule and shielded from life itself.

But water is able to provide and protect only when it is in its natural state. Water in nature tries to return to its natural, structured state. Water works upon itself; in a river, the water is working on itself, constantly cleaning and structuring itself. The river has geometric forms in it—boulders, rocks, and ridges. As the water tumbles through these forms, it is swirled in multiple directions. If you take a gallon or ten gallons of water and dump it in a mountain stream at the top of the mountain, and then collect it at the bottom, the water is structured.

Flow form devices basically duplicate the process of the river by providing the specific geometric forms. By running water through a structuring device, in a very short period of time, you allow the water to structure itself.

The Structured Water Unit is a multiple vortex. It makes the water spin in both directions simultaneously, multiple times. The vortexing allows the water to structure itself. Water is the machine; there are no chemicals, no magnets, and no moving parts. The water itself is the moving part. The device just brings the water to that place of being free to do what it's meant to do.

The common water filers in everybody's homes are devices you have to constantly tend to. But an Ultimate Structured Water device is a one-time investment. You buy it one time. You put it on whatever water source you choose, and it will never wear out, because it has no moving parts.

The Structured Water Unit goes on the first entry point of water into the home; it's an inline device and it's bi-directional, so it doesn't matter how you put it on. The installation process takes about a half an hour.

It's just a matter of measuring the pipe, cutting the pipe, and slipping the structuring device in between. From that point on, all the water that has passed through the device will be structured. Structured water will go into all the pipes in your house, through your water heater, and into every place that you use water.

When you have a Structuring Water Unit on your home, it provides everything with structured water: your ice machine, your gardens, your plants, your animals, your swamp cooler, everything that uses water will be using structured water. You'll notice that everything takes less water when it's structured—about 30 percent less water. You'll be drinking it, bathing in it, and eventually it will go down the drain, back into the sewers, and—if you live in a city—the water will go back into the processing system. It may even enhance that system.

The next thing you might notice is that your water heater will start dropping all the sediment that's built up; all the aggregates, such as the calcium build-up, will drop to the bottom of the heater. You might have to flush it occasionally in order to eliminate that stuff.

Structured water will also change you. Because what are you? You are probably 80 percent water. As we age, that percentage of water drops—unless you're drinking structured water. Then the percentage will stay the same. Water is involved in almost every bodily process, and this water must be replaced. Distilled water and RO (reverse osmosis) water is *hungry* water. It has no power to discern what is good and what is bad. It takes it all.

But structured water naturally assimilates the things that are bad for life. Chlorine is bad for life. Fluoride is bad for life. All toxins are bad for life. The water you drink from this small Structured Water Unit will have any toxins that are present locked away in a form that can't harm you—and if there is still room in the water molecule, it also will start pulling away those things in your body that are bad for life, as it's passing through you. It will detoxify your body. Structured water *only* pulls things from the body that is bad for life. It gives freely and fully all the things that are good for life.

Structured water is free of memory. It has a balanced pH. Structured water is that it is absolutely balanced. And it's the balance of nature that brings us to that place of doing what we are meant to do and being what we are meant to be.

Chapter 2. An Interview with Inventor Clayton Nolte

Structured Water: the 10 pointed star in Sacred Geometry

A woman came into our center. She'd been there before, so we were familiar with her. However, this time when she entered we immediately noticed some changes in her.

Close to age seventy, she previously had a somewhat dried appearance, like an autumn leaf before disintegrating. Papery-thin, dry. Today she had a vitality about her, an excitement and energy. Her skin appeared more nourished. Her wrinkles were no longer prominent. Her hair was silky and curly, even better than with a fresh perm.

"I have something I want you to try," she announced.

Uncovering what appeared to be a glass of water, she asked me if we had smaller cups for tasting the liquid. After we produced some, she poured the water into each cup and encouraged us to drink it.

Curious, we first looked at the remarkably clear fluid. Sniffing, we noticed a lack of odor. No chemicals, like chlorine. No natural sulfur smell. Nothing.

So we tasted it.

It seemed to flow through my mouth and down my gullet like slow cool molasses, spreading an incredible soothing lightness through my mouth and down.

Was this JUST water?

We began to eagerly gulp it until each glass was empty. She smiled at us and began to tell us about this water.

"It's called structured water. It goes through a cylinder like a filter, but it's not. Any water can go through this cylinder. And what happens is all the toxic chemicals get transmuted, leaving only the original pure state of water," she said.

"I don't know how it works, but the inventor is in town, selling them out of his car. I'd like to get him here to talk about it," she suggested.

So would we. Curious, we asked him in for a private interview and a public presentation on this 'cylinder' that structured water.

Before he arrived for either one, I got on the internet to see what I could find out about Clayton Nolte or structured water. There wasn't much.

I was, however, able to order a shower unit. I wanted to see for myself what this thing did before I was influenced by Clayton or anyone else.

Easy to install, the shower unit is bi-directional, meaning you can't make a mistake in installing it. It works in either direction and is just as effective either way. Unscrew the shower head from the pipe. Add the shower unit to the pipe. Add the shower head to the unit. If it hangs too low to shower comfortably, add a riser pipe first.

The first time I showered in it, I felt my body immediately relax into the pure, clean state of what felt like living water. No chlorine smell, just silky, moving water. It was like standing under a gentle waterfall, or even a home-made, outdoor shower using collected rainfall. It felt soft and pure.

"Thank you!" I heard and felt my body say.

Soap didn't seem to foam as much, but I didn't feel I needed it to.

My skin and hair felt hydrated, smooth, and silky afterwards, even in this dry Arizona air.

During the day and subsequent days I noticed that any daily intentions I recited in the shower manifested faster and more profoundly.

From, "I am a living field of love and light" to "I choose to release anything not for my highest good and healing and fill myself with love and light" to "I choose to release any stored toxins from my bodies, with grace and ease, and imprint whatever higher frequencies will prevent me from taking on any more."

And so on.

It was incredible how the days flowed effortlessly, in harmony. How happy my body was. How happy all my bodies were.

My cat refused to drink anything but structured water. So did we, as a matter of fact. Even if it came from the tap initially. We NEVER drink from the tap. We've always gotten our water from the live spring twelve miles away. But just running water through the garden unit or the shower unit creates a better tasting glass of water, more hydrating and energizing than anything I've ever tasted.

We left town for a week. I watered plants with structured water before we left. When we came back, the jasmine plants had doubled in size and had more blossoms than ever before. The almost dead aloe plant had a new lease on life, with seven new leaves. All in one week!

We went to a local restaurant. New owners had spruced it up quite a bit, and the food tasted much better. Then we noticed a sign on the table saying they used structured water for their drinking water. As we looked around, we noticed how joyful the atmosphere was. People at different tables were talking to each other, apparently meeting for the first time. Diners were going back for seconds and thirds from the delicious buffet.

What was going on here?

When Clayton Nolte came in for his interview, the first thing he said was, "Everybody has what I have. Everybody. But they haven't taken the time to practice, to observe, to be present. That's what it's all about."

Raised on a farm in Minnesota, he went to college for two years, studying engineering. At that time, he wasn't sure which area of engineering to go into, so the University gave him a battery of tests and determined the Air Force was a good choice.

In the Air Force, he received the same battery of tests, and then talked to some men in black suits who profiled him into research and development in electronic warfare.

"I received a broad range of education, and a lab with an unlimited supply of toys and tools, and it ended up to be quite an experience," Nolte said. He added that he's taken a leave of absence in the last ten years.

I asked, "So what began your journey with water?"

"It's simple. Water appeared where it should not."

After a moment of silence, I asked the logical question: "Where was that?"

"In time, the observation of structured water was there in this world of pollution," he said. "My journey was in studying nature and the things that man can do, but are not practiced."

So how does this work exactly?

"The Ultimate Water™ units themselves are pretty basic. There are no moving parts, no chemicals, no filters, no magnets, no electricity needed to run this. The inside is glass and Sacred Geometry. Sacred Geometry has to do with everything. It IS everything. Basically this unit helps water to go back to its perfect structure that it has in nature. Structured water has a life force energy. Anything good for life is carried on the outside of the water molecule and easily assimilated. Anything not good for life is pulled to the inside of the molecule and shielded. So life becomes the filter, passing through and going back into nature.

Structured water has a balanced spin of counter-rotating fields. The more balanced the spin, the more equal, the more pure the structure. Living water in its natural state has the same counter-rotating fields. All I've done is create a balanced field so water can remember its natural state."

I just looked at him.

"You all want an explanation! You want to intellectualize it. You want a mathematical formula for it all. But in nature, the true balance is the key. We need to let go of HOW," he said.

"Water in its perfect structure takes on a God form. It's magic. When water is in the process of structuring, it doesn't see anything else. It's just enamored with the possibility of being free.

"Structured water can't survive in man's world. Everything man-made is injurious to life. No matter the amount of structured water, or what type of pipe is used, structured water will not live beyond 300 feet in straight pipe. So if you have a whole house unit, you need to know the location of your pipes and their relationship to each other in order to know if you need one or two units.

For example, there was a man who ordered a house unit. His plants in the front seemed to thrive, but he still noticed hard water spots on his dishes from the dishwasher. When we investigated, we found that he'd put the whole house unit by the water main, as instructed, but he had two hundred feet of driveway! The three hundred feet rule seems to be very consistent. It's just the way it is. Once he installed a second unit closer to his kitchen, he was very satisfied with the results.

"In nature, there's always a however. In ten miles of pipe with structured water in the pipe, if you have a shut off at one end, all ten miles of water will be structured within minutes. Water entrains within minutes, both forward and backward within the pipe.

"Structured water is highly stable. It frees excess oxygen. It supports aerobic bacteria and kills anaerobic bacteria. Consuming structured water instantly hydrates the cells. In the QXCI machine, you would instantly see the results in twenty-two seconds, from the time you think you're going to pick up the glass and drink from it. What happens when you drink tap water is, your body expends around one hundred KW of energy to be hydrated. With structured water, your hydration is instantaneous and your energy can do what it's meant to do. It resets your DNA and RNA back to before circumstances and pollution.

"Once a plant is given structured water, it receives far more nutrition from the air. Once it contains its predisposition of source and vitality, then regardless of pollution, it can receive its life force from the air.

"Placing structured water, a container of structured water in the environment will pull out negativity and toxins from the environment. It will structure a glass of non-structured water just sitting close by."

I said, "I noticed I was releasing more cellular memory...."

He nodded. "I recommend asking the universe to erase all demands, prayers or anything you haven't received yet. Just erase it. Because eventually, when you get to that 'free space.' the first thing you ask for could manifest instantly. Because you're no longer being weighted down by the universe trying to provide something you had to have when you were thirteen years old. And believe me, everyone who's practiced letting go of things without knowing what they are, those people are very empowered.

"Structured water gives people greater potential or opportunities to know what's theirs—to be given dominion—to no longer be susceptible to anything taking you off your center."

I asked about Masaro Emoto's work with water crystals. "Did you also find the perfect hexagon shape?"

"Yeah, sure," he answered.

"Intention works also. With what you saw, was it comparable to Emoto's work, as in love and gratitude creating beautiful crystal shapes?"

"Comparable yes. But you know the word hexadecimal or hexagonal implies something that's only temporary. **You want your water to look like this? Be like this. You can make everything that way.** Why should I make it for you? Be that way. There are people in this world who can instantly manifest anything they desire. Even you can do that. So…you have no excuses."

I said, "It isn't about that, it's about empowering the individual. What you're doing with this device is helping individuals to empower themselves so they can do more."

"Right."

He continued with sacred geometry. "Everybody thinks water is a hexagon shape, but it's not. *The actual figure, in my experience, is a ten-pointed star. Two intersecting pyramids.* The actual figure points on a pyramid are four on the bottom and one at the top. Drop it in point to point and you get a ten pointed star.

From those ten points, it can morph into anything. In electronic form, the ten-pointed star is a device of changing dimensions, for inter-planetary travel. It's just energy powered by intention. That's just the way it is."

"I see hydrogen as the aspect of the Father. Everything turns on hydrogen. It's the first part in all elements, in all things. Oxygen is the Mother. And carbon is the child," he said, in a remarkable connection to the Unity Breath Meditation. "Everything is a combination of these three. Everything."

What are some of the miracle stories you've heard with structured water?

"There was a 75 year old man with life-long eczema who bought a shower unit. Within 18 hours, 90% of his itching, burning skin irritations had disappeared. Another man had esophageal cancer. He was hospitalized with severe dehydration, and given no chance of survival. His friend began bringing him structured water every day. He walked out of the hospital in under four weeks, in remission. Another person with cancer began drinking the water, and within three weeks, was in remission. The list goes on and on. I hear miracle stories all the time."

What is the longest range of effects you've studied with the structured water units?

"Well, I've been making these units for more than fifteen years, and people that first bought them from me are still happy with them. Nothing has been replaced, or needed fixing. There's no moving parts and no filters to replace, and the lifetime guarantee seems to be working."

What are the other benefits of structured water?

"It tastes better because it structures any chemicals natural or man-made, anything that is toxic, and just surrounds it and releases it. It just passes through your body without effect. So the first immediate effect is your body heals from the polluting chemicals you've been used to. Increased vitality. Less joint and muscle pain. More energy because there's more oxygen. Increased absorption of vitamins, minerals and medications. Vigorous plant growth. Less fertilizer required. It removes existing calcium and aragonite deposits.

No hard water spots. Less cleaning required for kitchen and bathroom. Prevents and removes corrosion and increases the lifespan of pipes, hot water heaters, dishwashers, swamp-coolers, water heating systems, ice makers, etc. The list goes on and on. Less algae growth in ponds and lakes, cleaner fish tanks, healthier pets, improved crops and garden growth, better tasting food. I could go on and on."

Are there any negative effects from the units?

"Well, once you start using this on your garden, be prepared to always use it. Birds and other wildlife will demand it. Plants will demand it. And if you live in an area like Arizona where javelinas run wild, you'll have to protect your garden device from them. They'll find a way to destroy the garden unit. It's like they have to have whatever life force energy is coming from there.

And the units will break down in prolonged sunlight. The outside is PVC pipe, so find a way to shelter it. If you're in a cold zone, don't leave water in it when it starts to freeze. Take it inside. Also, at this time, we don't have the units fitted for metric pipes, like Europe. But we're working on that."

So what's next?

"In my research, I want to get to that place where no one has been. Where there are no words. There's nothing you can't do if you have enough money and you have people who aren't limited.

"Take what you know and be in joy. That will catapult us into what we can do to make a difference. We have to be ready for that. In my journey, the greatest propulsion is taking action. There are organizations all over the world where there are think tanks. But the truth is in action."

In love, joy and gratitude,

Phoenix Rising Star

Chapter 3. Natural Action Structured Water Machines

The Natural Action Structured Water Devices Structure Water for a Healthier Life in The Same Way Mother Nature Does!

You will feel energized from these incredible units.

The Natural Action Structured Water is the Best Water Balance Available!

And that's just the beginning

Once you taste the water you will never want to be without it

Your body will feel incredibly energized

The innovative Natural Action *Structured Water Units* work without chemicals, filters, salts, electricity, or magnets. Best of all, there are no moving parts or complex metal alloys.

The Natural Action *Structured Water Units* are truly maintenance-free, water structuring systems.

But here's the most important part!

*The Structured Water **Unit raises the pH to 7.0-7.5, the balanced hydrogen potential for a long healthy life. To make sure you always have balanced water when you travel, there is also a portable** Natural Action Structured Water **Unit that can be carried with you so you always have balanced water.***

I'll let you in on a little-known secret: Despite what you may have heard — much of the tap water, deionized water and even bottled water has a pH of around 5.5-6.5. The long-term effect of this acidic water is that it causes the buildup of free radicals in the body, which are the source of aging, cancer and the destruction of healthy cells. Filter systems that remove almost everything from water also remove water's aliveness, leaving one with essentially "dead" water.

But that's just the tip of the *iceberg. The* Natural Action Structured Water *Unit* softens water while leaving in all the healthful minerals standard water softeners and reverse osmosis systems remove.

But you probably wonder how this unit does all these things

Let me show you exactly how this works. This exclusive technology uses an advanced understanding of the vortex phenomenon, utilizing the dynamic characteristic of water itself to create a naturally balanced **structured water** that works at the molecular level. It alters the molecular structure of the water, activating and retaining the healthful benefits of minerals and characteristics while excess suspended solids, contaminants and sediment are dynamically isolated or removed. The specially tuned geometry of the unit creates an energy environment for water to structure itself. This gives water a lower surface tension and better hydrating properties, which can help in both your external and internal environments. Super-hydrating water will help open up clay soil conditions in landscape, and it also will isolate negative dissolved solids from harming your body's cells, leaving you with a balanced, healthful body.

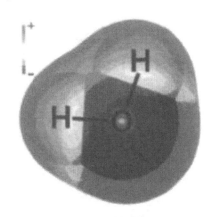

Approximate shape and charge distribution of water.

What's more—and this is important—the geometric configurations within the unit break up large, low-energy water molecule clusters into smaller, high-energy clusters. This eliminates negative energy patterns (sometimes called the "memory" of water) and redefines the water's natural healthy energy pattern. You may notice this effect while showering with and drinking structured water.

NOTE: More details on the various Natural Action Structured Water devices invented by Clayton Nolte are provided in Chapter 10.

Chapter 4. Health Benefits of Structured Water

Water inside our body's cells is structured water. The water preferred by human cells is structured into small clusters containing 5 to 20 molecules.

Even small amounts of contaminants, much lower than levels now considered safe in our water, might have detrimental biological effects. This brings us to look at the allowable contamination levels in all our water sources. We may have been damaging our bodies and our environment much more than we could have possibly imagined.

If water can retain the memory of the pollutants, and that memory can survive filtration and chlorine treatment, what information is this water giving our body's cells?

There are regions of the earth where water is thought responsible for the longevity of the local people. The Hunza Valley in northern Pakistan is famous for longevity. Also, the waters of Lourdes in France and other venerated sources are reputed to have restorative qualities.

The waters of Tiacotle, Mexico have been praised for their health-giving properties. What is it about those waters that makes a difference? They all have the same thing in common. They all contain essential, bio-available minerals in solution. So, in that sense, the "miracle" waters are not absolutely pure.

These remarkable waters are, however, all free of disease-causing bacteria, so they are safe to drink. Yet these similarities do not account for their fame. We can make similar water in the laboratory, and it does not have any more benefits than normal water.

The reason these waters are so prized is that all of them have a different structure than most waters. Researchers had to wait until Nuclear Magnetic Resonance became available to show that these waters have distinct differences from other waters.

WATER IS THE:

Ultimate food * Greatest medicine

Most economical fuel and energy source

Good health is determined by the cells' ability to receive water. When the cells walls are no longer flexible, aging begins. A child's body is 86% water, but this water ratio is reduced to 65% as we age. Our brain is 96% water.

Extra-cellular fluid depends on more available oxygen.

Inner-cellular consumption depends on more available hydrogen, which is why maintaining a good pH balance in the water is so important.

Structured water and surface tension

Dehydration is the principle causative factor in aging and most diseases. This is why it is important to drink eight glasses of water a day and to abstain from drinking anything other than pure water. And it is vital to drink water with low surface tension. Surface tension is measured in "Dynes per cubic centimeter."

Distilled water is about 72-78 Dynes/cubic centimeters, whereas water necessary to penetrate the cell wall needs to be less than 46 Dynes. The reason alcohol is so easily absorbed by the body is because its surface tension is 28 Dynes. The *Structured Water Unit* produces microclustered water with a surface tension level below 46 Dynes, which makes it super-hydrating.

Retaining healthy minerals

Water Structuring technology that utilizes nature's own methods produces cleaner, softer, more vital, better tasting water without using chemicals, salts, or complex metal alloys. It is a truly maintenance-free, total treatment, water conditioning system. This system softens water while leaving in all the healthful minerals the body needs and which standard water softeners and reverse osmosis systems remove.

This system's process uses the dynamic characteristic of water itself to create a "*Structured Water Unit*" that works at the molecular level. The

27

units alter the molecular structure of the water and the minerals in the water.

The healthful benefits of the minerals are made available to life while excess minerals, suspended solids and sediment are dynamically removed.

Going beyond existing systems, this Natural Action *Structured Water Unit* employs an innovative application of an advanced understanding of the "Vortex" phenomenon. This water restoration process separates contaminants, while simultaneously restructuring, re-energizing, and reactivating the water itself.

The special waters associated with longevity and health are rich in bio-available minerals. More than fifty studies in nine different countries have shown an inverse relationship between the amount of magnesium in the drinking water consumed and heart attack rates. In areas where magnesium levels are high in the drinking water, there are fewer heart attacks; where magnesium is deficient in the water, there are more heart attacks. **Distillation, R/O and water softeners**, the most popular forms of home water treatment, get rid of most *or all* essential minerals. Some bottled water manufacturers replace these by spiking the water with minerals, but are those the essential minerals that are in the array supplied naturally by flowing water? Nature knows what is best for life. There is no man-made magic bullet that can equal what nature supplies, because nature is more in balance with life itself.

Structured water vs. pollutants

Structured water has the ability to attract and encapsulate, within the water molecule, elements that are bad for human life. When this water is consumed, it attracts more of these elements as it passes through to the elimination system. Elements good for human life ride on the exterior of the water molecule and are released into the body's function.

Structuring water is nature's way of removing excess minerals and suspended gases from the water. This helps to revitalize the water and make it cleaner and better-tasting so that it can hydrate the cells better. Structuring lowers the surface tension so the water is better suited for cleaning and mixing. It also increases the Potential Hydrogen (pH) to 7.2-7.5, which is or more alkaline; such water can remove the built-up scale in plumbing and fixtures. Structuring gives water a lower surface tension and makes it more hydrating, which allows it to help carry off internal toxins.

In well units, structuring more efficiently removes excess minerals and suspended gases, including sulfur smell. The efficiency of the unit and the well, being ground water, is exponentially enhanced when the heavy discharged water is returned to the source of the well, through a process called 'entrainment,' which causes all the elements to return to their family — their source.

Hydrogen, the fuel of life

Structured water is loaded with negative hydrogen ions, and "Hydrogen is the fuel of life." All the food we eat does one thing for us: it releases hydrogen, which is burned by oxygen in the final chemical reaction, releasing the energy that makes ATP, the fuel that actually runs our bodies. Carbohydrates are one-third carbon, one-third hydrogen, and one-third oxygen.

We have enzymes in the body called dehydrogenates whose purpose is to loosen hydrogen on the food we eat so that the hydrogen (hydrogen is the fuel) can be burned by oxygen, releasing energy. The carbon and oxygen left on the carbohydrate turns into carbon dioxide gas, which we breathe out and the plants breathe in. This is called the Krebs cycle.

Hydrogen is the energy source that runs our bodies; it is the energy source that fuels the universe; and it is also the energy source that runs the sun. Hydrogen makes up 90 percent of the mass of the universe. Albert Szent-Gyorgyi, a Hungarian physiologist, said that hydrogen is the carrier of electrons in the living system, and that no electrons are carried anywhere in the living system unless they are attached to hydrogen.

Hydrogen is the carrier of all electrons in all chemical reactions. Cells, proteins, and tissues in our bodies store hydrogen in huge quantities in such a way that you don't need enzymes to use that hydrogen. Szent-Gyorgyi also said he believed that hydrogen had something to do with cellular division itself and might be the secret of cellular division.

Structured water offers many benefits

There are many benefits of using the structured water produced by the Natural Action Structured Water Unit, which balances water in the same way Mother Nature does.

The Natural Action Structured Water *Unit* was designed to geometrically structure water so that living things can use it best. The body seeks balance, and water also seeks to be in balance, so the body will replicate itself to water which is naturally balanced. Nature's gift to humanity is water, structured to be self-healing and in balance. Water is also attracted to balance. As water has memory, it will remember all thoughts and energies in its immediate surroundings, both negative and positive, in its effort to achieve balance.

Nature accelerates this process in the environment by creating the geometric configurations necessary to achieve and maintain balance, through the vortex activity created as it moves over stones, waterfalls, and ravines. This is why water purifies itself as it moves downstream or is fed by high elevation glacial runoff. It also explains why water moving through as little as 300 feet of pipe, or which is held in a bottle for a long period of time, becomes 'dead' water.

Structured Water Unit Health Benefits Include:

- It assists in the release of vitamins and minerals healthful to all life
- It makes water more fresh-tasting and invigorating
- It improves the taste of coffee and juices
- Fish tanks become cleaner and healthier
- Ice cubes are harder and clearer
- Hair and skin rinse cleaner and hair feels better when washed
- Livestock, domestic pets and fish become healthier
- It improves health, less joint and muscle pain, more energy
- Increased Potential Hydrogen (pH) 7.2-7.5 balance
- Increased absorption of medications, vitamins, and minerals
- Less soap is necessary when washing

- No more irritations from pollutants (chlorine, etc.)

- Reduces the effects of sunburns

- Prevents dry itchy skin — no chlorine smell

- Promotes longer life and slows aging

- More refreshing showers and bath, replacing soft water units

- Reduces odors around/in bathrooms and toilets

- Clothes are washed and rinsed cleaner in the laundry

- Removes existing calcium and aragonite deposits, providing spotless dishes, window washing, and car washes.

LANDSCAPING AND OUTDOOR WATER FEATURES

Nature also geometrically structures water so that balanced water is available to the environment. The Natural Action Structured Water Unit creates a Fluid Machine that alters the molecular structure of the water, activating and retaining the healthful benefits of minerals and other health-giving characteristics of the water while excess suspended solids, contaminants, and sediment are dynamically removed. This creates "wetter" water that can penetrate the soil, carrying sodium, magnesium, and other elements deeper into the soil. This allows greater water penetration in the roots and fewer salts which bind the top soil. Some of these benefits are:

- Cleaner hot tubs and spas with less chemicals required

- Improved ability of plants to withstand lower freezing temperatures

- Cut flowers last longer

- Healthier landscape — greener lawns, more vibrant trees & shrubs.

- Improved growth of crops with increased biomass (27% to 40%)

- Healthier household plants

- Reduces the amount of water required (up to 50%)

Chapter 5. Cost Savings of Structured Water

COST SAVINGS

There are also numerous financial benefits to utilizing the structured water for both drinking, livestock watering and crop and landscape growing:

- ▶ Less soap is consumed when washing

- ▶ Less fertilizer is required on gardens, house plants, crops and trees

- ▶ Removes corrosion and increases the life span in pipes, hot water heaters, dishwashers, swamp-coolers, water heating systems, ice makers, etc.

- ▶ Improves aerobic bacterial activity in all septic and sewage systems, reducing anaerobic bacteria

- ▶ Eliminates polluting salts, chemicals or corrosive by products

- ▶ Reduces the amount of chlorine required for swimming pools, hot tubs, and spas

- ▶ Slows algae growth in ponds and aquascapes.

- ▶ Increases longevity of all systems that use water

- ▶ Removes existing calcium and aragonite deposits in pipes, water heaters and faucets.

- ▶ Increases profits from sales of coffee and juice

Chapter 6. Environmental Advantages - How Structured Water Helps the Planet

It Has Infinite Possibilities!

Structured water well units can more efficiently remove excess minerals and suspended gases including sulfur smell. The efficiency of the unit and the well, which draws ground water, is exponentially enhanced when the heavy discharged water is returned to the source or well. This process is called Entrainment and it causes all elements to return to their family - their source. As a result, all wells using this same source ground water are enhanced and eventually they will produce water as clear and clean as if there were a unit on every well.

1. The exchange between nature's systems always creates a surplus of energy.

2. Water exists within almost every religious system as the expression of mans connection to the inner harmonies and rhythms in nature.

3. Man became dysfunctional with the harmony of nature during the advent of civilization.

4. Water is the great mediator between the energetic and material worlds, between the realms of pure light and matter.

5. Water has no inherent form of its own; water embraces the form of everything it comes into contact with.

6. Water becomes the carrier of life, the chief communicator channel between life energies.

7. Water is the accumulator, transmitter and transducer of energies and is continually transferring life processes from one system to another in its helical evolutionary manner.

8. The connection with water was lost by man when he turned away from internal insight, which comes through nature's

rhythms and the energy of life cycles around us.

9.   Explosive hydrocarbon technologies are robbing the earth of its oxygen resources at an alarming rate.

10.   The wonder of oxygen, with its ability to capture and transport non-vectored or feminine quality life force energies, is our single greatest resource.

11.   **The depletion of oxygen overshadows all other pollution concerns.**

12.   **Water has the ability to hold memory through its geometric structuring.**

13.   A very simple test for measuring anomalous water is its freezing points. Structured water freezes at a lower temperature.

14.   Structured water increases minerals, medications or any other supplement absorption to 100 percent.

15.   Through the process of entrainment, Structured Water continues its life giving properties long after its intended use.

16.   Assimilating Structured Water requires no physical energy.

17.   Structured water, in its perfection, knows what is good for life and what is not by the negative and positive charges on each component

18.   There are 66,000 pollutants that can be dissolved in water.

19.   Water becomes dead water when run through 300 feet of straight pipe.

Chapter 7. Examples of the Benefits of Structured Water

Benefits of Ultimate Structured Water in a Dairy

(Reprinted with permission from Adam Abraham of Thought for Food, http://phaelosopher.wordpress.com/ and http://www.photonicwater.com/)

Structured water affects bio-photons and eliminates staph bacteria for raw dairy

Here is an excerpt from a post on the "Thought for Food" blog originally titled "History in the Making: Bio-Photon Presence in Structured Water Confirmed."

Jackie and Athena, from "Save Your Dairy" where they water their cows with "structured" water. Since we've been discussing water in connection with the Site 41 controversy, it's doubly interesting to come upon this report which connects water quality with raw milk and which even ties it all in with Fritz Albert Popp and his bio-photon research:

"Getting a handle on this structured water concept can be a challenge for linear, "show me the numbers," left brain-dominant people. Evidence is there, mind you, but you sometimes have to look for it differently.

As a first impression, upon taking my first shower with structured water, I noticed that it feels "wetter" than what was coming out the showerhead only minutes before. I now understand that this feeling is what is generally referred to as "soft." This is one indication of smaller cluster sizes and higher density and hence greater oxygen content in the water. Structured water shows great promise as a salt-less water softener. And as this missive moves along, you'll see another area of great potential.

Another piece of evidence of higher available oxygen content in structured water is in how it affects living things that don't have intellects and egos. Plants and animals qualify as part of that population.

A simple test was to simply take a couple of plants and water them, with tap water, and with water that has been structured. We did this with basil, actually purchasing three pots and a pack of seeds, which were planted. One pot was watered with tap water and another with structured water (run through the kitchen faucet that has an under-sink unit installed).

The water of the third pot had first been warmed in the microwave, cooled off with some ice, and then applied to the planet. While it did sprout, seedlings were sparse. It never thrived, and in a short period of time, was gone.

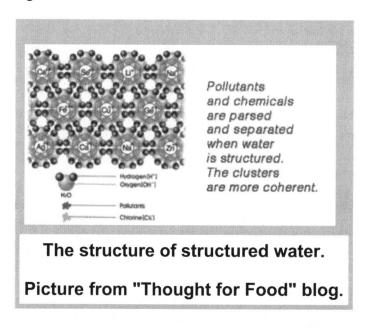

Pollutants and chemicals are parsed and separated when water is structured. The clusters are more coherent.

The structure of structured water.

Picture from "Thought for Food" blog.

The surviving plants grew up in the summer heat of central Arizona, where the ground surface temperature is easily enough to fry eggs by day, and perhaps run "slow cook" food by night. Yet, during this time, the both plants pushed through the surface and formed according to design.

The plant that was nourished with structured water eventually grew larger, and proved to be the more robust of the two. Structured water vs. tap water, with the resulting difference in plant growth. Thought for Food photo.

STRUTURED WATER   TAP WATER

Buoyed by these developments and looking for more, I contacted a friend who owns the only dairy producing raw, unpasteurized milk in the state of Arizona. Jackie C. is the one who originally brought Sally Fallon (Weston A. Price Foundation), and Mark McAfee (Organic Pastures) to my attention. Both eventually became guests on my radio show, with my Organic Pasture's visit being part of my first road trip in 2008 to Northern California.

Raw milk producers walk a tightrope. They produce a balanced, nutrient dense food that contains real vitamin D, live enzymes, and beneficial bacteria, the stuff that antibiotics kill off, but that prescribing physicians rarely concern themselves with replenishing. Yet, when you read a raw milk label, you're informed that since the product is not pasteurized, it "may contain organisms injurious to your health."

This is enough for most uninformed people to put the raw milk down (where it's available), and get the pasteurized milk. Yet, pasteurized milk labels don't say that it contains synthetic vitamin D, and has no natural digestive enzymes, nor any live aerobic bacteria. Did you read the recent Washington Post article stating that 70% of children through young adult are deficient or insufficient in vitamin D? We have cultivated such deficiencies into the behaviors that are encouraged and discouraged. Government enforced pasteurization of dairy products, including the "organic" variety, are woefully lacking in real nutritional value that actually contribute to human health. On the other hand, if they're allowed to sell at all, producers of products that do help, such as raw milk and dairy products, are forced to include misleading labeling that most consumers won't take the time to see beyond.

Perhaps it is for that reason that Jackie C. named her operation, Save Your Dairy (www.saveyourdairy.com). However, she was excited about the prospects of learning about structured water, and after meeting Clayton Nolte, the device's inventor, agreed to install two units, one that would structure the water that the cattle drinks…"

You can see the structuring unit just below the pump in the above image.

Another unit was installed to structure the water that is pumped to a holding tank that supplies all the buildings on the property. You can see a close-up of the device in the picture below.

"….I visited the dairy last week and talked to Mick, who manages the facility. They observed an immediate change in drinking patterns. The cows drank less water. The herd (130 head) had been drinking around 1,800 gallons of water per day for several days. Then, consumption would spike to over 4,000 gallons, then return to the lower level. After the structuring devices were installed, water consumption leveled off to around 1,800 gallons each day.

This would support an expectation of improved hydration, as the cattle drink according to thirst, and stop when that thirst has been satisfied. While this was a pleasant, and you might say 'positive' outcome, it wasn't enough for Mick [to] consider the structuring devices had a significant impact. The real issue was that the water source that his cattle draw from, a nearby well, was believed to [be] infested with a strain of Staphylococcus bacteria.

According to Wikipedia, Staphylococcus, which include aerobic and anaerobic forms, can (as an anaerobe) cause a wide range of diseases in humans and animals either through toxin production or invasion.

The now famous term "MRSA" stands for Methicillin-resistant Staphylococcus aureus, a bacterium that no longer responds to beta-lactam antibiotics, which include penicillin and cephalosporins.

So Mick had a far greater problem weighing on his mind. If the well water was indeed full of Staphylococcus, what would the drinking water have? If the drinking water was full of Staph, then what good would a structuring unit be? Furthermore, the presence of an anaerobic microorganism in structured water would be counter-indicated, because structured water is optimal, and living.

The bio-photon energy that accompanies a structuring event manifests as abundant, stable oxygen. If the inventor's statements were true, then there should be no Staphylococcus in the herd's drinking water.

When I visited, the lab tests were still out, so we discussed possible 'Plan B' approaches to bacteria control that would not require pumping the animals with antibiotics. One option was adding MMS — sodium chloride — into the water supply. The chlorine dioxide generated would oxidize the anaerobic microorganisms in the drinking water, producing no carcinogenic byproducts.

It was a moot point by that afternoon. The lab results were in. The lab confirmed the presence of Staphylococcus in the well water, but found ZERO bacteria in the structured drinking water sample. He was one excited dude! No bacteria, produced with no antibiotics! Jackie is now the owner of the first dairy in the world to produce structured milk!…"

On the heels of this development, an order came in for a Ultimate Water garden unit. Destination, Elzweiler, Germany, about 130 km southwest of Frankfurt. It's amazing and gratifying to see how people from around the world are learning of this technology, as well as paying the prohibitive import duties — obviously set up to deter trade between nations — in order to avail themselves of the structured water experience.

Now I remind you that you can structure water. Each human being can, and is a water-structuring agent. The caveat is that we must be in a joyful, loving state. When we perceive ourselves as being "stressed out" we leave our structure hat at the door, and are at the mercy of whatever we feel vulnerable to. A water structuring device allows us to gain the benefits of being conscious of our innate power and using it, even when we aren't.

Within two weeks after that unit shipped to Elzweiler, a surprised Clayton Nolte, the unit's inventor, received an email from the excited buyer, who indicated he had done tests on the water that flowed through the structuring unit. He said that a device they use to measure bio-photons had confirmed said emissions in water that had passed through the garden unit. They were gearing up to purchase more units of different sizes in order to expand their research.

This was good news, even encouraging news, but not necessarily GREAT news, that is, until Clayton sent a copy of the report to me. Printed the front page was the name Fritz-Albert Popp. This didn't mean anything to Clayton, but it rung a bell with me.

The study was titled, "Elektrolumineszenz von Wasser" which I take to mean "electro-luminescence on water."

Abbildung 1

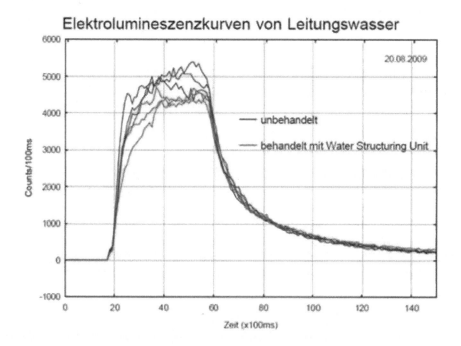

Elektrolumineszenzkurven von Leitungswasser

The researcher explains:

Blue graph lines are normal tap water and red ones are structured water-we use the water in Prof. Popp's laboratory, where I directly connected the unit to the water source. Distilled water would show effects in the same way, which means that our water has capsuled the micro-particles into clusters, so they can not react anymore to strong polluted water would have a higher score, because it has more dirt (micro-particles) inside, which makes the water more electrolytic -- more biophoton emisson-higher score!

In this researcher's paradigm, less is more.

I mentioned being familiar with the name Fritz-Albert Popp, but initially, wasn't sure where. It was from reading *The Field: The Quest for the Secret Force in the Universe*, by Lynne McTaggart. She devotes a chapter to his work, and includes numerous additional references throughout. Having your work independently and excitedly confirmed by a world renowned bio-photonic researcher is a great way to start the day.

I eventually found an excerpt from *The Field* on Albert-Fritz Popp and read it to Clayton, so he could further appreciate the significance of the point in time that we have reached.

A new doorway has opened a tad more, as structured water history moves on. The implications of Staphylococcus (or any anaerobe) without resorting to antibiotics, by using less to achieve more desired results, is mind-boggling, if enough people like you and me wake up. When we stop fearing nature, and actually return home, we have much to learn, and to gain. And just perhaps, we can live in better health for less, which I'm sure Senator Kennedy would have preferred.

Also read this paper "Raw Milk is Alive" on applications of Fritz Albert Popp's work on bio-luminescence to raw milk quality assessment.
Lead photo from Save Your Dairy website. Other pictures from Thought for Food blog.

Current water treatment systems only take the junk out of water; they were never designed to remove the 'memory' of junk that water retains. That 'memory' may be doing harm in the long run.

Benefits of Structured Water in a Greenhouse

Transcript of Adam Abraham Interview with Roger Dagget
(Reprinted with permission from Adam Abraham of Thought for Food,
http://phaelosopher.wordpress.com/ and http://www.photonicwater.com/)

ADAM: A lot of people are asking the question what is structured water and why should I care? More specifically, why should anyone believe that a device that relies on no external forces, such as magnets, electricity or filters, could actually effect water quality in any measurable way? Some answers are easier to demonstrate than they are to explain.

With that in mind, I hit the road. We're on our way to a greenhouse outside of Coolidge, Arizona between Phoenix and Tucson. We're going to meet Roger Dagget, whose impression of the Utopic Water Device began with some amazing cucumbers that his greenhouse yielded. But it didn't end there. In addition to an amazing yield of cucumbers which originally got his attention, Roger noticed some other effects of his change to the Utopic Water Device which, if we didn't know better, might even be considered mystical.

And by the way, by the time we learned of these amazing cucumbers, they were already at market and had been sold. So as it turned out, the cucumbers were just a beginning. Roger starts off by showing us some promising results he is experiencing now with tomatoes.

ROGER: What we're attempting to do is grow high nutrient value produce. We use a refractometer to measure the nutrient density of our produce. Our objective is not to grow so much high volume produce as you can see we have here, but to make sure that each piece of produce that we have is full of nutrition.

ADAM: I am going to interrupt and ask why is that a problem? Is there some question about nutritional value that we're not aware of? That is what I would like to know.

ROGER: When I started this project 9 years ago I started in the water end of the business and I started working with structured water clear back in the year 2000, and after I figured out how to structure water the next question that came was how do we build the soil? The water will carry the nutrient to the soil but what is our base for soil? I looked for the answer from one coast to the other.

Finally I came up with the equation that said it doesn't matter how green, tall and bushy a plant is, what matters is the nutrient density of the plant. You can measure that with an instrument called a Refractometer, and it gives a reading called Brix. I started testing the produce I have been buying at high, high retail prices, all organic produce, high prices, and I was depressed for 30 days because they were all low nutrient density. I got low readings on the Refractometer.

ADAM: So they looked pretty?

ROGER: Looked great!

ADAM: Everything was great, they were priced high, as you would expect from something that had those good looks, but you also assume it has some nutrient value, but really the most important aspect of it was missing.

ROGER: Right, that being the nutrient density. So the long road started. There are several iterations and this is where we have ended up. We have had some growth explosion here, because if you look over here, here is the trellis wire and this is row number 1 and row number 2, row number 3, row number 4. These are 83 inches in height right here.

Now, the game plan was that row number 1 was supposed to go right here and this is where it would grow. And then we put row number 2 here. As you can see, row number 1 has expanded clear over here into row number 4, so we have got double the growth that was anticipated, based on the paradigm that was shown to us to grow by.

We also have an error down here (indicating). The recommendation was to put the tomatoes eight inches apart. I knew I was going to have a little more energy than the eight inches so I put them a foot apart. And you can see even at a foot apart we came in so dense that they actually cannibalized each other; you can't tell where one plant begins and the other one ends.

You can see we have a tremendous amount of tomatoes set here. The really good news is I have only had three of them turn red so far, and one of them Brixed out at 12.2. Now, my goal was to get to 14. Whether any of these get to 14 or I don't know, but I tested tomatoes from one coast to the other and never got one in double digit. I have talked to people that have had double digit tomatoes but I never personally tested one.

Most of the tomatoes I have tested out of the local gardens around the Coolidge area here have tested below 5. That is why I was depressed for 30 days, because I paid five bucks a pound for tomatoes and they were virtually below par.

That is one of the reasons that we have such a health crisis in the United States today and why it is so hard for people to stick with a good diet because when they give up their Big Mac and they give up their Hostess Twinkies to eat the tomato or carrot, they get one that has got such low nutritive value that they don't experience a change in their health and so they say why keep doing this?

ADAM: That's true, and there is a trust factor, there is a fiduciary factor from the producer's standpoint. We're going to these stores, buying and specifying these types of products with the expectation that they have in them what nature has intended to be in them, and yet when it becomes an acceptable practice to irradiate these products or do other types of things and still call them organic, then a huge disservice is being perpetrated.

ROGER: Absolutely. The exciting thing about it is the first Refractometer that I got that was used over at Bottled Water Images cost $5,000. I sent it back to the manufacturer to get it calibrated to make sure it was working, and talked to them, and that is how much that unit sold for new.

Today, just like everything else in the world of technology, you can buy a wonderful little Refractometer that is much simpler to operate and just as accurate and it costs you $300. So there is absolutely no reason for anyone not to have a refractometer. You can actually get the analog refractometer today for under $100.

And it is just like everything else. The country with a longest life span on the planet is Japan and where are these units coming from? Japan. They understand Refractometers in Japan. You're not going to fool them with the produce. They all check it over there. And that is a place where we need to get here today to solve our health care problems.

ADAM: Let's talk about the cucumber plant that you have. This is exciting.

ROGER: I just threw a few cucumbers in for the fun of it, and I did a watering on a foliar spray of the cucumber on a Saturday, and I had used the structured water and I had used a humus product and I applied it, and I usually don't come to the greenhouse on Sunday and so it was Monday morning when I first came back to the greenhouse.

I walked in and I looked at that cucumber and it looked like an excited cucumber. It was standing up just like this! And I go holy smoke, so I got the trellis string out and I said we got to run this puppy up.

So I continued to water on a daily basis with the structured water. We give it some compost tea and some other formulas once a week, the foliar feed with the structured water, and the cucumber got to a height of over 15 feet. From that cucumber plant I harvested in excess of 56 pounds of #1 cucumbers! This doesn't count the juicers that I took off of there that we just juiced because they didn't turn out perfect. So 56 pounds.

Now, Briden Big Charles and I were over at Mesa College by invitation at their Ag Department and we Brixed the cucumbers that they were growing there and they barely got over 1 on the Refractometer scale. Mine didn't get to 14 where I wanted but they were over 6, so we had 500 percent nutrient density over what they are growing at the college there. So 56 pounds; a whole lot better than what you can get at the grocery store cucumbers. Some of them were two pounders. And they tasted good - they weren't bitter. That was the great part.

ADAM: You had some other effects from getting this structuring device on line. Talk about that.

ROGER: I cannot quantify on this side of the unit that the water made these better per se because I didn't have a control or whatever, even though we got great results and I wouldn't take the unit off for anything.

But Clayton, the guy that builds the unit, told me when he was telling me about the unit that it would not only program the water on the outlet side of the unit, it would also program water on the inlet side of the unit, the feed side of the unit. Needless to say I didn't believe a word he was saying but I put the unit on anyway. It has got to program water on the feed side.

So three things that I have noticed out here. Number 1, I have an old mobile sitting over there, and domestic engineering is not my strong suit. It has a restroom in there with a toilet and it hasn't been scrubbed for quit some time and there was a tremendous film building up in the bowl. One day I noticed in there that the film was starting to lift. I'm the only one out here 99 percent of the time and I haven't been scrubbing the stool. Well, long story short, it finally hit me two or three days later it has got to be the water that is starting to pull the scum, the film off of the side of the toilet.

Now, over here on the other side we have an RO unit. You know it is two 4 by 40 membranes in there. I have been working with 4 by 40 membranes since 1994 when I got the first water store, and those have to be cleaned two to three times a year, depending on usage and feed water.

Now the membranes I have run at about 130 pounds pressure. When the pressure gets up to 150 pounds, you have to clean the membranes or you have to replace them. When you clean the membranes it is nasty chemicals and a nasty job and I don't like doing it.

ADAM: When the pressure goes up, does that mean they have sediment?

ROGER: When the pressure goes up it means your membrane is scaling, all the stuff you are trying to take out of the water is finally plugging up that membrane. The water pressure is going up.

So I said I'll come back and clean you next week, since that is my favorite thing to do. I came back a week later and in 15 years I have never seen a membrane de-scale, but the pressure had gone from 150 back to 130, which is normal. 130 is where these membranes want to be running. Different types of membranes run at different pressures, but these run at 130 for the volume I want. It had gone from 150 to 130, so it de-scaled the membrane.

Now remember this on the feed side of the unit. This is what really amazed me about it. Also I have a water wall here and I have a sump outside that we run the waterfall out of.

It is not a good tank to have outside, it is a clear tank and it grows a lot of algae in there and you have to be diligent about taking care of it or it really gets bad. I was remiss. I walked out there one day and you couldn't see two inches into the tank it was so green and murky. You know my favorite thing to do is clean, "I'll clean you next week".

I went back a week later and I could actually see the bottom of the tank. Hadn't done a thing. So when you read all the literature about how the water works and it tells you what it will do, you think that is hard to believe, but then when you experience it, you see the membrane de-scaling, you see the tank cleaning up, all on the feed side of the unit, that I can quantify.

ADAM: Now two other things; one of them had to do with fire ants. What happened?

ROGER: Again I can't contribute that all to the water but when I bought this property the guy I bought it from, one of the first things he handed me was a can of something ... I forget the name of it but we had a tremendous fire ant problem and I would pour some of it in on the hole and the next day they would all be dead but three days later there is a new mound of them over there and a new mound over there and all over the place, and you can drive around through the neighborhood here and see them. And I just noticed -- I don't how long ago it was, 90 days ago, I said I haven't seen any fire ants around here lately.

And so what we have done is we have changed the energy pattern of the property here, because the insect comes, the rodent comes to take out what we shouldn't be eating. So the energy levels have changed here and they have left. I can go over to my neighbors and show you the fire ants, they are still over there, but on this property here, four acres, I haven't seen fire ants for at least 90 days.

ADAM: I know what the other thing was. The fact is you have had a structuring device online before putting this unit in, so a lot of these conditions were still present even with the other structuring device.

ROGER: The other structuring device I have had excellent results with, especially in the area of water savings. We have demonstrated that and had a couple different projects that we can save a lot of water by using this unit, but like you say the unit was on and the membranes have been scaling all these years with that unit on. And so the only time the membranes did not scale was after we put this other unit in.

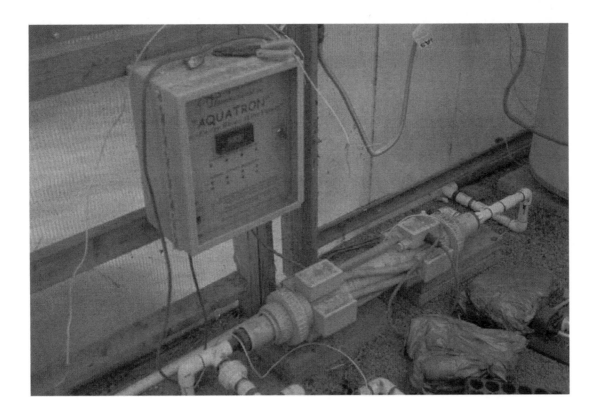

ADAM: We are talking about something that is totally green. It sounds hard to believe when there is no electricity, no magnets, nothing other than movement that is making something happen. And sometimes experience is the best way of really demonstrating what is possible.

ROGER: I still think there is a synergy effect of everything that we do, from the microbials that we propagate to the water that we use to just our attitudes; everything is energy. But definitely the water has contributed to the higher energy level that we have.

ADAM: Especially when you look at the other structuring device you had. Were you using the same types of like the humus and the other ... were those constant before?

ROGER: No. I'm fortunate that a lot of the things were but I had two variables come into play, the water and the humus. Both came into place at about the same time so I hadn't used those before.

ADAM: That is a good thing too. The nice thing about nature is that it is complimentary, they work together. It is not an antagonistic kind of situation where one thing is going to come in like the cavalry and do something to the bad guys; there is a synergistic approach.

The water should be there. The minerals, the other aspects that the humus or humic or fulvic acid or whatever they are, they should be part of that too and they all work together to actually create what you are looking for. Thank you very much.

ROGER: You bet.

ADAM: I want you to thank ROGER for sharing his experiences with the Utopic Water Device and my friend George Clark, a nutritionist and founder of Back Fence Nutrition, for joining me on this journey. You could say that Roger Dagget's story is one in 6 billion and you would be right, but it holds a key that is important to us all. Everyone needs water and everyone needs water that contains life, that contains energy, and water that has biophotons released that has been measured, a measurable increase in biophotons is water that has life within it. And in Roger's example you see what is possible. The changes that will occur for you are yours.

If you have any questions or if you have a Utopic Water experience that you would like to share, please contact me at Adam@TalkFor Food.com, and if you are interested in more information about a Utopic Water Structured Device, please contact your distributor.

NOTE: The Structured Water devices invented by Clayton Nolte are available from Adam and from Ultimate Destiny Network, PO Box 20072, Sedona, AZ 86341. Phone 928-284-2671.

Chapter 8. Comparisons With Other Processes

Current water treatment systems only take the junk out of water; they were never designed to remove the "memory" of junk that water retains. That "memory" may be doing harm in the long run.

Current water treatment systems go to extremes, such as distillation, to create absolutely pure water; they take all beneficial minerals out of the water. Many bottled water products are treated in this way. Drinking nothing but distilled water may actually leach some essential minerals from our bodies; distilled water is considered "dead" water. Most modern water distilleries were designed long before the structure of water was considered important. They produce pure but energetically "dead" water.

Not only can complex filter systems remove almost everything from water, they also remove water's aliveness. The **Natural Action Structured Water Unit** removes unwanted sediment while leaving in the minerals and characteristics that are essential elements to water that is "alive."

These are some of the water treatment systems, presently in use: 1) Reverse Osmosis, 2) Flash Distillation, 3) Electrodialysis, 4) Deionization and 5) Ion Exchangers (Soft Water Tanks).

Reverse Osmosis (RO)

Reverse Osmosis (R/O) is very popular today but R/O removes all beneficial minerals from the water. It also wastes three out of four gallons of water in the process. The most prevalent of present systems pushes water through micro-porous membranes that are meshed sufficiently fine to prevent the passage of most dissolved solids.

This removes approximately 50% of the salt as well as other solids with each pass. R/O processes water for small water units placed outside grocery stores as well as the domestic water supply for small metropolitan communities. The wastewater from R/O units in some places is so concentrated with salts and other minerals that it become a threat to the good bacteria in septic systems.

One of the major disadvantages of reverse osmosis is the large amount of brine discharge that, in some cases, will have deleterious effects on enclosed bays. It can kill fish and other aquatic life. A second, subtler negative effect of R/O is the demineralization of water for human and animal consumption. This water becomes known as 'hungry water', which may have the initial benefit of cleansing the body of unwanted toxins. However, prolonged use can demineralize the body, weakening the immune system.

Distillation

This process evaporates the water and then recondenses it, leaving behind the dissolved solids. This process can be less costly, because unlike reverse osmosis systems, distilleries do not need to be periodically closed for reconditioning. Distillation can refine the water to as little as 10 mg/l dissolved solids, compared with R/O's 50% reduction per pass. But flash distillation creates the same problem of brine water, which must be drained or hauled off. Another disadvantage is that volatiles, such as methane

Electrodyalysis

Electrodialysis, like reverse osmosis, also employs a screen, but in this case electrical energy is utilized. The electrodialysis process lets the salt through and keeps the water back. This is the opposite of reverse osmosis.

Deionization

This process involves the use of resins that carry either a positive or negative charge. These resins draw the elements to them and remove them from the water. They are easy to install and inexpensive for small manufacturing or laboratory use. A major drawback for high volume use is that they must be recharged either by washing the resins with acid or exchanging them after as little as a thousand gallons.

ION Exchangers (Water Softeners)

Some cat-ions will easily exchange with other ions under certain conditions. An example of this would be a soft water tank, which uses sodium-saturated salts to exchange sodium for calcium and magnesium. This system is valuable where corrosion in pipes and calcium build-up on enamels, such as household appliances and swimming pools, is of concern. Ocean water is 80% sodium, 8.5% magnesium, and only a fraction calcium; it's not usable for human consumption or agricultural use because of the sodium. Conventional water softeners increase salt levels in our tap water. When you shower with ion-exchange softened water, it is feeding these salts to the largest organ in your body: your skin.

Ion-exchange resin water softeners—that is, most water softeners—also remove all beneficial minerals in the water as they add a great deal of sodium or potassium. They put out waste water that is incompatible with septic tanks because, if you kill the bacteria, septic systems don't do their job. For this reason, many states have banned the use of water softeners for homes with septic systems.

Kangen VS Structured Water

By Brydon Big Charles of Utopic™ Structured Water

I must start out by sharing with you that I am very familiar with the Enagic Corporation, as I was involved in their company and used to own one of their $4,000 counter-top models. If fact, I still do own it; however it is not in use. It took me six or seven months to release my attachment to that machine, because I had spent so much money on it. That unit only filtered the water at the kitchen sink and didn't address the all the rest of the water sources in my home. By contrast, Ultimate Water uses a technology that took care of all the water in the home, did not use electricity, and never had to be serviced. There were no limitations as to the amount of water that it could structure—and all for a quarter of the price!

As you might imagine, this was a hard pill to swallow after I had been sold so well on the absolute necessity of a Kangen machine. As I began to open myself up to the Ultimate Water technology I began to understand the actual difference.

From hereon in, I will call it ionization. Ionization is a process which uses electricity to electrocute the water. This can only happen because of the mineral content that is in the water. We cannot ionize distilled water because distilled water can't conduct electricity. Throw in a little salt and a little calcium and potassium, and the water will sizzle and fry.

Most people do not realize this, but any water ionizer is, in essence, a hydrogen fuel cell. The electricity is poured onto the metallic plates and, because of the mineral content that is in the water—meaning the minerals are attached to the water molecules and clusters—the current goes through the solution, tearing apart the most natural and essential relationship on the planet: H2O. Water by itself does not have an ionic charge. Once you add minerals, which have a bi-polar ionic charge, the water is able to be ionized.

So here we have the most balanced, natural, and harmonious relationship in the world—one Oxygen and two Hydrogens atoms—being ripped apart by a manmade outside force called electricity. The end result is that you have a mixture of frazzled H2O's and OH-'s and some free-floating H's. This is how the pH of water becomes increased.

I used to take fresh Kangen water to my grandmother every day or every other day, from my condo to her retirement home. After making a few trips, we began to notice that there was a pile of hard calcium on the inside of the water bottle. I had questioned its presence; my sister, I believe, said "oh, just rinse it out with 2.5 acid water and it will come right off," which, of course, it did. I began to study why this would happen and the answers slowly revealed themselves.

During the sales pitch that I had received, the Kangen rep had told me the story of the memory of water and how the Kangen machine would erase and clear all that. I was also told that Kangen means "to return back to it origin" in Japanese. I am not sure if that is true, about the meaning of the word in Japanese, but I know for a fact that the Kangen filter does not fully clear the memory of the water. If water remembers everything, and it just came out of a chamber where it was electrocuted, do you think it just may remember that? If you think not, then perhaps a good experiment would be for you to stick you tongue in the light socket and flip the switch to see if you can remember it yourself—because, remember, you are 75% water.

Each time, I would have two gallons of frazzled water, OH-'s and a pile of Hydrogen bubbles that had the fresh memory of being electrocuted in a glass container sitting in my truck, which contained excessive electronics. As I would start the vehicle and the electronics began to blast electromagnetic frequencies through the glass bottle, it triggered the freshest memory of the water and caused the free-floating hydrogen to return to the natural union of H2O. When this happened, the calcium that was attached to the H and OH-, which was used to do the electrocuting in the first place, became precipitated out to the inside of the glass container.

Now this was where I started to really scratch my head and think. If it will do that to the inside of a glass bottle ... then what is it doing to the inside of my body, or the bodies of loved ones with whom I am sharing this water? The answer was that it was doing the same. All it takes is one single transmission of a cell phone in the pocket for that natural relationship to re-unite after the process of ionization. And I don't think it is possible to simply flush our system and arteries with 2.5 acid water to get rid of the build-up of hard calcium deposits.

Another interesting thing that any ionizing organization does not tell you is that you MUST not drink high pH water an hour before, and a least and hour after, you eat. As we eat our food, our stomach uses acid to digest what we put into our mouths. If we dilute that acid with high pH water, we are simply sabotaging our own body's natural ability to break down and absorb nutrients from the food we eat.

The next point I would like to make is about the farce of needing to drink high pH water to offset dis-ease. It is true that much dis-ease does flourish in an acidic body, but we have to break it down to a cause-and-effect basis to get to the true source of the disease.

1) Cancer grows in an overall acid environment in one body.

2) Did the cancer cause the acid or the acid cause the cancer? Neither!

3) Cancer and acid are just two regular dudes hanging out with each other because they are two effects of the same CAUSE.

4) The true cause of all this is emotional dis-ease ... aka fear. Please follow . . .

Un-dealt-with fear is the basis of all disease known to man. Fear is only meant to be a natural messenger. It is meant to alert us of a potential danger and that is it. We are supposed to address the fear, thank it for its message, and then release it as we proceed with caution. In nature, how many times to we see and animal get startled and then spend the rest of its existence in therapy for the fear that it holds onto?

We never see that, because the animal releases the message that alerted it in the first place. We, as humans, will continue to hold onto things that we only meant to get our attention or to make us aware of what we need to do. In our holding on to fear, we are sending a signal through our bodies that continually shouts "PREPARE FOR TAKE-OFF!"

This signal puts our adrenal glands into overdrive and causes then to continually produce adrenaline. A big part of adrenaline is called cortisol, the body's rocket fuel that allows us to get out of harm's way. Cortisol is useful if we burn it all up. However, if we do not use it all up, it just sits in our body and then creates an incredibly acidic environment!

The very little slightest thought or worry of fear will cause our adrenaline system to kick in. A good way to monitor whether you are living in stress (fear) or not is to notice the way that you breathe. If you are a chest breather, that means you are too stressed and your adrenals are kicking out cortisol.

If you are a stomach breather, that means that you not stressed and your adrenals are resting. Notice the way that an infant breathes, from the stomach, without a care in the world.

When a person is in cardiac arrest and they are having CPR administered, the reason that their chest is being pumped is because the body has a built-in mechanism: with the rise and fall of the chest, it will shoot adrenaline to the heart to get it kick-started again.

When we are startled or frightened, we can often feel our hearts race and pound at the bottoms of our throats. That is because of all the adrenaline rushing to the heart, causing it to pound without us even moving.

The most effective way to change the pH in one's body is to simply have an attitude adjustment which would include not allowing outside influences to trigger us and put us into that fight-or-flight / fear state. This deals with the issue at the source of the problem.

To come at disease by trying to fix it with diet and drinking water is simply beating around the bush. All pH's are just the effect of whatever caused it. You can NEVER change the cause of an effect by altering the effect. You may affect the effect, but that is just temporary.

The water current from Ultimate Water replicates what nature does to water in the hydrologic cycle of water flowing down the mountain steam and through the aquifer—which, by the way we do not allow to happen anymore, as we never allow the water that we use to fully go through its cycle.

The Ultimate Water technology has no moving parts, just as water is the only thing that moves in the mountain stream. Ultimate Water technology uses no electricity, as it is not natural for humanity to use electricity in any way, shape, or form.

Ultimate Water technology employs multiple, spherical flow forms that are spaced in specific geometric patterns, which cause the water to vortex equally in all directions. When water is spun, it causes anything that is of a different density than water to separate out. And there is only one thing that is the same density as water in this world, and that is water. Because of this, everything else that is in the water becomes structured onto itself.

Most of us can remember spinning in circles as a kid and then stopping really fast, only to fall down because our energy field continues to spin while our bodies stop. That feeling of dizziness occurs because the polarity of our energy field is going against that of our bodies. The same happens with all the properties in the water. The calcium no longer has an ionic charge and cannot attach itself to itself or to any surface.

When Ultimate Water dries, the calcium becomes an inert powder that can be easily blown or brushed of. If there is excess mineral build-up in the pipes of your home or in your hot water heater, with in two to four weeks, it will all be gone. Now, if it will do that to the pipes in your home, it will most definitely do it to the pipes in your body (arteries). Plague in the arteries, put simply, is nothing more than calcium deposits.

By far, the biggest difference between the two technologies is a famous phrase and title of an outstanding book *Power vs. Force* written by Dr. David Hawkins. Within this highly recommended read, the author describes how he can find and calibrate the source of any and all things to either be from a place of power or a place of force.

Anything that is found to be of force is considered to be negative for life, and anything that is of power is on the positive end of life. It also equates to different levels of consciousness, meaning that the higher the number, the higher the consciousness. When things are found to be coming from a place of power, it is evident that they occur with ease and grace. On the contrary, things that are of force require exponential amounts of energy.

With ionization, the electricity is a force that tears apart the water cluster. It is an external force or an outside influence on the water. Structured Water, on the other hand, is created because of a power that is unleashed from within the water molecule. This power (bio-photon) helps overpower the electromagnetic bonds that attach all the minerals and other physical properties in the water.

As you can see, one technology (ionization) is using force (electricity) to treat the water while the other technology (Ultimate Water) generates a natural power (chi energy) from within the water, which is then able to support the nature that is in all life.

Chapter 9. Technical Data

All Living Organisms Contain Structured Water

Water inside our body's cells is structured water. The water preferred by human cells is structured into small clusters containing five to twenty molecules.

What is good, healthy water? It must be fit to drink, and be free of pathogens and pollutants. Municipal water in most cities is treated to make it safe to drink. The treatment, normally chlorine, kills most disease-causing bacteria. That's a good thing; however, many people consider the levels of chlorine in the water to be a pollutant. It also tastes bad. There is big business in chlorine-removing filters. It seems we have taken the lesser of two evils in disinfecting of our water. The treatment eliminates the threat of bacterial contamination—

But does this make healthier water?

And what is structured water? Water molecules are attracted or loosely attached to each other through hydrogen bonding. In normal water, this attraction makes water "cluster" together in large groups of molecules. Both the size and shape of these clusters can affect biological organisms.

The water molecule, made up of two hydrogen and one oxygen atoms, is what most of us think of as "water." The true picture is a little more complex. Water molecules appear to be very gregarious. They like to get together and are seldom found alone. They will cluster into groups of from five molecules to more than six hundred molecules. These groups are not static.

Water molecules will switch from one group to another very easily, and do so often. Hydrogen bonds are being made and broken several times a nanosecond. This creates the unimaginably dynamic energy environment of water. It is the size and shape of these clusters of molecules, in their never-ceasing interaction, that is the "structure" of water.

The "***Natural Action Structured Water Unit***" is a new technology for water treatment that utilizes nature's own methods, producing cleaner, better tasting water without the use of chemicals, filters, salts, electricity or complex metal alloys for a truly maintenance-free total-treatment water conditioning system.

This new technology employs an innovative application and advanced understanding of the vortex phenomenon utilizing the dynamic characteristic of water itself to create a "***Natural Action Structured Water Unit***" that works at the molecular level. This **Machine** alters the molecular structure of the water, activating and retaining the healthful benefits of minerals and characteristics, while excess suspended solids, contaminants and sediment are dynamically isolated or removed.

Specially tuned geometry creates an energy environment for water to structure itself. This gives water a lower surface tension and better hydrating properties. This geometric technology breaks up large low-energy water molecule clusters into smaller, high-energy clusters. This systematic treatment eliminates negative energy patterns (sometimes called the memory of water) and redefines the water's natural healthy energy pattern. Structured water allows us to imprint through the DNA and RNA the knowledge of its secret blueprint. By doing so, it can help us to become balanced in the universe.

Chapter 10. Examples of Natural Action Structured Water Devices

Natural Action "Peace and Tranquility" Structured Water Shower Unit

"When I take a shower with my Ultimate Structured Water Shower Unit, it feels like I am enjoying being under a waterfall. It is a peaceful and tranquil experience that I cherish. I take an extra shower unit with me whenever I travel. I am proud to be a distributor for Ultimate Water!" -- Cindy Shields, Edmonton AB, Canada

The Natural Action Structured Water Unit can be installed in the shower for softer skin and all the advantages attributed to a soft water installation, without the deleterious results of the ion exchanges or brine water. It can also be a multi-use for filling water dispenser jugs or drinking glasses. In most showers this requires a special riser pipe, screwed into the stand pipe to lift it above the head.

The Shower Unit is the smallest of all the units with a basic length of 6 ½ inches and with connector 7 inches and is shorter again because it is at the point of contact with your body with instant hydration. If the shower outlet is too low a 10 inch riser should be available at a local hardware store. This unit is most popular -- you can get full hydration and fill your water bottles too.

Benefits of the Natural Action Structured Water Unit:

- Hair and skin rinses are cleaner and hair feels better when washed

- Less soap is necessary when washing

- No more irritations from pollutants (chlorine, etc.)

- Prevents dry itchy skin — no chlorine smell

- Promotes longer life (anti-aging)

- More refreshing showers and bath (replaces soft water units)

- Reduces odors around/in bathrooms and toilets

- Removes existing calcium and aragonite deposits

The Natural Action Portable Structured Water Unit is the answer when you want to enjoy the benefits of an energy infusion when you're out and about, whether around town, at a local restaurant, or on the road.

Important Information and Ideas for Usage

IMPORTANT:

1. This device is not designed for extended hot water use above 140 degrees.

2. This device is not designed to sustain freezing temperatures with residue water inside; unit may crack and/or function will possibly be deteriorated.

3. ***Do not drop - function may be deteriorated.***

4. The unit you received may rattle, this is normal; it contains a geometrically tuned chamber with specific geometric forms that align with the direction of flow.

5. The unit is bi-directional but pouring into the funnel end is easiest.

6. The unit will become brittle and may deteriorate desired function if left exposed to the sun for an extended period of time.

IDEAS FOR USING THIS UNIT:

7. When traveling, use for structuring your drinking water.

8. Structuring juices of any kind (apple, grape, grapefruit, etc.) brings more flavor to the juice.

9. Small enough that it can be taken to a restaurant to structure your water and any other beverages you order.

10. Structuring a lesser quality wine makes it much smoother tasting as if it has aged.

11. Structuring alcohol that has an edge to it will smooth it out.

12. Use the unit as a conversation starter – Offer to structure someone else's beverage.

13. Use your imagination and tell us *your experience* of using this device!

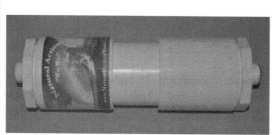

Our new *'Ultimate Structured Water'* is producing amazing changes in our water! My skin feels soft and lubricated after bathing. I use less soap and shampoo. Less soap is needed for washing the clothes. The new water has rejuvenated our plants. My husband says our water tastes better too; and morning coffee is smooth – no longer bitter. We love the new structured water machine and the new life it has produced in our water.
-- Lileth B. Randall, SLC Utah

The Under Sink Structured Water Unit comes with the connectors for adapting it for installation under the sink. The basic unit is 8 ½ inches with a connector of 10 ½ inches. It is bi-directional and can be mounted in any direction. This unit is shorter than the *Whole House Unit* because it doesn't have to deal with the restrictive conditions of the entire house.

When showers and landscaping are not a consideration, the under-the-sink unit is a perfect installation. It is designed to be used in place of filters, R/O units and charcoal filters. The filters can remain if debris and sediment is a problem.

However, these are very seldom needed and can remove beneficial minerals (dissolved solids) contained in the source water. This unit dispenses water in the optimum manner for the balanced water to reach your body in its optimum structure, through the cold water outlet at your kitchen faucet.

This will give you the best taste, maximum absorption of the water through the cell membranes in your body and the greatest health benefits of naturally balanced water. It is easily installed by anyone with minimum plumbing experience.

There is usually a small pipe underneath the kitchen sink which can be removed on the cold water side. A flexible hose on each end of the unit is connected to the two exposed ends where the piece has been removed. A bracket is included to brace the unit against the side or back wall. This unit is also advantageous for anyone living in a rental unit because it can be easily removed and the old pipe can be replaced. Then it can be reinstalled in another rental unit or home.

www.ultimatestructuredwater.info/undersink_unti.htm

Natural Action Structured Water Garden and Landscape Units

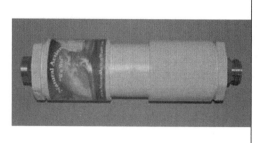

The **Garden Structured Water** unit is equipped with garden hose connectors for gardens, motor homes and portable uses and is the same dimensions as the Under Sink unit. This unit is shorter because it doesn't have to deal with the restrictive conditions of the entire house.

The Garden Unit serves as a portable unit. It is for a person on the move who wants to be able to have balanced water wherever he or she goes and is also appropriate for someone who is renting and does not want to permanently install a unit in the home. Structured water is most effective when consumed as close to its source as possible.

Structured water has memory and will incorporate the vibration of its immediate surroundings. Although it can be stored in five gallon containers for dispensing at a water unit, it tastes and feels best immediately after it is processed by the **Structured Water Unit**.

The Garden Unit meets all these needs. One end can be easily and temporarily screwed onto a garden hose faucet outlet. This method is preferred when filling a container for a drinking water dispenser. Keep in mind, there might be slight changes in the effectiveness of structured water over time or if it is stored in a plastic jug.

At the other end of the unit there is a fitting for the end of a garden hose with a sprayer. If the water is filling containers for drinking, the unit should be attached directly to the outlet faucet or there will probably be a slight taste of the rubber hose picked up by the structured water. This will not affect the garden watering as the structured water retains its alkalinity, micro clustering, oxygen retention and reduced surface tension. It will break down the hardpan soil, leaching harmful salts deeper into the soil.

The result will be healthier plants and a reduction of standing water. Eventually, your garden will require less watering—from 10-50 percent less, depending on individual soil conditions. The unit can be easily transferred from one garden outlet to another.

If levels of calcium, magnesium, and sodium, as well as chlorides, sulfates, and bicarbonates—as a group or individually—are too high, plant growth can be hurt. High levels can even cause plant desiccation or poor growth. We often blame this on poor soil structure.

Plant and tree growth reductions, as a result of dissolved substances in the soil, are similar to drought-stressed effects. An osmotic gradient on salty soils is formed. Water uptake by plant roots is increasingly restricted as the concentration of soil salts increases. Because of this, as soil salts build up in the soil, more frequent irrigation is necessary to help flush out salts and reduce water stress, often resulting in pudding and wasteful runoff.

Acidic soils make successful gardening difficult. The alkaline water emitted from the *Ultimate Structured Water* units alters the topsoil, making it more conducive to growing healthier plants.

Bliss Cafeteria, Sedona, AZ

BEFORE

"We were forced to replant the vegetable garden after realizing that our plants would not sprout due to large amounts of calcium in our well water system. The calcium had created a hard crust over the soft soil making it impossible for sprouts to penetrate through."

SACRED HEALTH, Sedona, AZ

AFTER

"We connected the Garden Unit to the hose and began watering. About this time I left town for 9 days and while I was away we continued to water the garden with the *Ultimate Structured Water*. When I returned the garden had not only sprouted but many of the plants were already 6 inches tall! After 5 months we have more veggies than we can eat. Also, we have noticed that we do not need to water as much, the plants absorb more water because of the lower surface tension of the water after passing through the device."

The Natural Action Structured Water Unit increases percolation in the soil, carrying the buildup of harmful salts into deeper areas. It reduces water usage for landscape watering and eliminates puddling and runoff. Because of its reduced surface tension, it prevents hardening of the surface soil. Sodium and other harmful salts percolate into deeper levels, resulting in deeper root penetration and hydration availability at those levels. This reduces the need for artificial fertilizers, pesticides, and other chemicals—and less water is required.

www.ultimatestructuredwater.info/garden_backup.htm

Natural Action Structured Water Whole House Unit

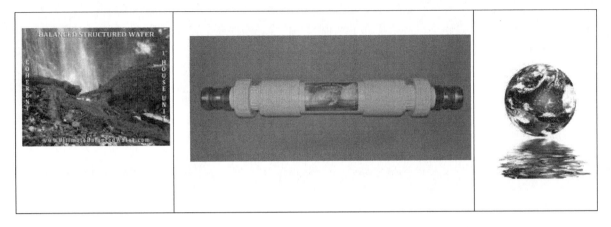

The Natural Action Whole Home Unit is for the person who wants the full effects of good drinking water, softer skin in the shower and bathing, the laundry, cleaner dishes and greater longevity of the water heater and plumbing lines.

The Greenest Choice in Water Softening!

• **No Salts**	• **No Water Waste**
• **No Magnets**	• **No Electricity**
• **No Maintenance**	• **No Brainer**

Make the green choice when it comes to choosing a Softener.

The Natural Action Structured Water units ensure the maximum life span of all water appliances in your home. Your ice maker, hot-water tank or tank-less heater, and dishwasher will operate smoothly without the build-up of harmful minerals. These units do not even use electricity as their design utilizes the flow of the water moving through the pipe as its energy source.

The Natural Action Structured Water Units have a maintenance free design which gives the home owner peace of mind that your investment will not be followed by ongoing monthly costs or practices that are harmful to the environment.

In addition to this, the Natural Action Structured Water Units produce a soft water that is safe to be consumed by all life. In fact a high vitality is gained by all those who consume it; humans, animals, fish, and plants. Irrigation applications can see a reduction of water usage of 25% to 50% while maintaining a healthier and more lush environment.

Soft water that is soft on the wallet and easy on the environment!

Being a skeptic by nature and profession, I am a scientist; I am leery of any claims that are put on a product. Show me the proof. When my wife first approached me on a unit that could be attached in line with our water system that would not only improve water but could actually improve our health I could only think she had been suckered in by a fast talking charlatan selling snake oil remedies. I agreed to have a unit (Structured Water) installed on the condition that it came with a money back trial if we were not satisfied. Thinking that this was a no brainier and we would get our money back I could save face and tell my wife "see I told you." Much to my surprise the first time I took a shower I had the sensation that I had used a conditioner on my head. Truly it could not be that on the very first use that I would feel results. I then decided to drink some and immediately on raising my glass to my mouth realized that it did not smell like our tap water. On tasting the water it was evident that it was different. I am not certain how it works, at least from a scientific point, other than to say that I understood the scientific reason behind the principal. Structured water is an apt name as that is exactly what it does. **I am so convinced by the unit that when I asked my wife what was it called she said that the product was so new that they had just recently named it. I told her that it should be called "miracle water".** I believe so much in the product that I have purchased additional units for all my family especially for my daughter who has a new born. **I would never return this product for any reason.**
-- Ed Chacon Archeo Astronomer 2008, Santa Fe, New Mexico

The Natural Action Structured Water Home Unit is easily installed in the water line this side of the water meter. The benefits from this installation is the unit's ability to give balanced water at each water faucet, remove unwanted chemical buildup in the pipes and other units as well as the benefits to either hand watering or sprayer units in gardening.

There is a slight disadvantage in distancing the drinking water from its source and some clogging of irrigation headers as the water removes scale buildup in the pipes. However, most people who have installed this *Home Unit* have not expressed any concerns with these.

The House Unit will cover the whole family dwelling indoors and out up to 300 feet of pipe and comes in a choice of ½", ¾", 1"or 1¼ inch in/out diameter water line. The ¾ inch basic unit is 11 ½ inches, and with connectors is 17 inches; the 1 inch unit basic unit is 11 ½ inches, and with connectors is18 inches. It is bi-directional and can be mounted in any position.

Benefits:

- Vibrant water at the turn of every tap in the house
- Increase of personal health and vitality
- Enjoyable bathing
- Happier and healthier pets
- Less mineral build up on surfaces
- Increase of cell hydration
- Smoother and fuller coffee and teas
- Crisper taste in cooking
- Spotless dishes from the dishwasher
- Extends life of the hot water heater
- Cleans the inside of the pipes
- Laundry is easier on your cloths
- Less detergents all round

Now, eliminate having to choose which faucet delivers you the water that your body really needs. The Home Unit is for the person or family that wants the full effects of high vitality drinking water, softer skin in the shower.

The benefits from this installation is the unit's ability to give balanced water at each water faucet, remove unwanted chemical buildup in the pipes and other units as well as the benefits to either hand watering or sprayer units in gardening. It even delivers high vitality water back to the public reservoir! It is also the most environmentally safe water treatment system as it wastes ZERO water and there are no filters to replace and dispose of.

The Home Unit is easily installed in the water line this side of the water meter. Some installs may be done by home owner if they are comfortable doing so. If homeowner is in question of the process we highly recommend *consulting with your local plumber*.

www.ultimatestructuredwater.info/home_unit.htm

Natural Action Structured Water Commercial, Pool and Spa Units

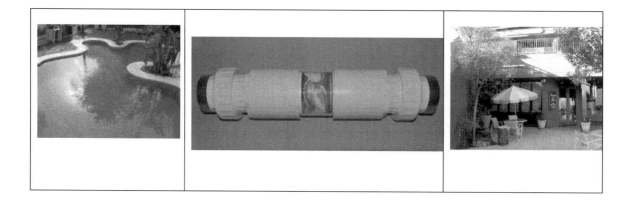

We are seeking potential experiential demonstration sites where visitors can enjoy the benefits of structured water such as retreat centers, healing and wellness facilities, and intentional communities.

www.ultimatestructuredwater.info/commercial.htm

Chapter 11. Questions and Answers

Frequently Asked Questions

We have received hundreds of questions regarding our Structured Water units and their use and application. This information is broken out into several categories and can be accessed through the Frequently Asked Questions menu above or through the links below. We also advise the use of the Search function located on the right side bar for quick results.

PLEASE NOTE: All data contained herein relates to structured water through movement (vortexing). It does not necessarily relate to structured water by other means (magnetic, crystals, energetic, etc.). Results from other forms of structuring may produce different results. In addition, none of the information provided is intended as medical advice. If you have concerns about your health, please seek the assistance of a qualified medical professional.

PRODUCT INFORMATION
This section provides answers to some of the questions we have received regarding the use of the Structured Water units.

INSTALLATION and PLACEMENT
This section provides answers to some of the questions we have received regarding the installation of the Structured Water units.

PORTABILITY and STORAGE OF STRUCTURED WATER
This section provides answers to some of the questions we have received regarding the transporting and storing Structured Water.

CONSCIOUSNESS and WATER
This section provides answers to some of the questions we have received regarding the consciousness of ourselves and Structured Water.

HEALTH ISSUES and WATER
This section provides answers to some of the questions we have received regarding the health and the possible benefits of Structured Water.

PROTECTION FROM EMF's
This section provides answers to some of the questions we have received regarding the effects on Electromagnetic Fields with Structured Water.

ENTRAINMENT
This section provides answers to some of the questions we have received regarding the entrainment of Structured Water.

Product Information

Question: We have a massive amount of iron in our water and our water is very hard. We put in an iron filter and a water softener. I have been learning more about water lately and am not comfortable with the water softener as I'm learning that it can be detrimental to our health and our environment.

I am interested in purchasing a unit for our home to replace the water softener. Is it possible to keep the iron filter and use your unit at the same time? We have 1 inch PAX piping. Can the unit be installed with that piping?

Answer: Structured Water units will work in harmony with all forms of water systems or filters. There may be some changes in the outcome but no worries. Structured Water will be highly accepted by all things (more on this if you desire). Our Structured Water units are adaptable to all types of water conveyance. Our units come with convenient optional connectors and full point by point instructions that may facilitate installation with ease. The included SharkBite connectors work well with PEX, CPVC and ridge copper.

Question: Are there different types of units for different uses? What do they cost?

Answer: There are currently five different Structured Water units available; the House unit will cover the whole family dwelling indoors and out (up to 300 linear feet of pipe) and comes in a choice of ½", ¾" or 1" in/out diameter water line. The ¾ inch basic unit is 11 ½ inches (with connectors 17 inches), the 1 inch basic unit is 11 ½ inches (with connectors 18 inches), the 1-1/4 inch unit is 17 1/4 inches with connectors, and all units are bi-directional and can be mounted in any position. All house units retail for $999.

The Under Sink Structured Water unit comes with 2 hose connectors for installation under the sink. The basic unit is 8 ½ inches (with connector 10 ½ inches). It is bi-directional and can be mounted in any direction and the suggested retail price is $349. This unit is shorter because it doesn't have to deal with the restrictive conditions of a whole house.

The Garden Structured Water unit is equipped with garden hose connectors for gardens, motor homes and portable uses and is the same dimensions as the Under Sink unit and the suggested retail price is $349. This unit is also shorter because it doesn't have to deal with the restrictive conditions of a whole house.

The Shower unit is the smallest of all the units with a basic length of 6 ½ inches (with connector 7 inches). The suggested retail price is $249 ($269 with the optional riser) and is shorter again because it is at the point of contact with your body providing instant hydration. This unit is the most popular as you can get full instant hydration with your shower and fill your water bottles too. If the shower outlet is too low, a 10-inch riser should be available at a local hardware store. The Commercial unit is designed for a 1-1/2 inch or 2 inch in/out water line with at least 50 pounds per square inch pressure is required. Its basic unit length is 13 ½ inches (20 inches with connectors). The suggested retail price is $1499.

Question: This is Linda. You spoke to Debbie and I on the phone a few weeks ago and she asked if the structured water unit would remove the heavy calcium deposits in her house water that is generated from their community well supply.

Deb ordered a whole house unit and a garden unit from me. She did not seem to get results when she hooked it to the outside faucet, so they hooked up the garden unit under the kitchen sink. Her partner is responsible for checking the purity of the community water so they had on hand a way to check the chlorine content. As far as they could tell the structured water unit did not take out the chlorine and when they boiled the water in a pan there was still a calcium deposit on the pan.

We installed out whole house unit a few days ago and simply love the water but we also have a carbon filter under the house to catch all the sand that we get from our city/lake water so we were not able to tell if the structured water unit took out our chlorine. My daughter installed her shower unit in St. Louis proper and got great results with no chlorine smell or taste and the water was "smooth" tasting.

Do you have any suggestion as to what can be the problem with Deb's water?

Answer: I could reiterate every statement I have made on these subjects but I feel it will be of no avail. My cynical response is "what you seek you will find". So with that I will turn these questions over to my associates who are all enamored by the wisdom gained through Structured Water in their lives.

Okay, so here's my take on it. There are 2 things at work as far as I can figure out. Any container or holding device for water already has a memory to it. Memory of its origin (ex: plastic) as well as memory of what has gone through it. So when structured water is first in this container or holding device, it may not stay structured for very long, depending on how long it's in this new container and how deep the cellular memory of that container is. However, that said, it will entrain itself and the container given enough time, say a month or so. I have witnessed this with my #7 plastic water container. At first, structured water tasted great, and within 24-48 hours, tasted like plastic. After using it continually with only structured water in it, the structured water now lasts more like a week, if I leave it there that long.

When you are testing for chlorine or any other chemical, you are using a test for chemistry. Structured water is not a chemistry. It is an alchemy. Structured water surrounds chemicals and helps them to be neutralized or not taken in by the body. The chemical is still there, but it is in a different structure. This is like testing for carbon. Diamonds and coal are both carbon. If all you are doing is testing for carbon, you will find carbon in both. That doesn't mean they are the same structure. With diamonds and coal, you can easily witness a difference with your eyes. With structured water and regular water, you can't necessarily witness a difference with your eyes, but you will witness a difference with your health and well-being, with your physical form and all your other bodies.

Question: So how do you test for a structure of water?

Answer: There is the GDV machine which acts like an advanced aura camera that takes pictures of the energy of the water. The structured water that Clay is promoting has the highest energy flow so far of any of the waters out there, including R/O, other filters, and other things claiming to be structured. I'm sure there are other ways of measuring structure, but we, the general populace, don't have access to them yet.

In any event, this is an opportunity to trust your inner guidance, listen to your heart, and observe any physical and emotional changes (or mental, etc.) and see if they make sense to you given the change in your water. If they do, great. If they don't, well, you have a choice of hanging in there long enough to entrain yourself and everything concerning this water, or not. Ultimately, it's your choice no matter what.

Question: My inox-steel heater has stains of calcium on the bottom, so it reduces calcium settlement – but not to zero – right?

Answer: Where the Structured Water is moving it will clear calcium within minutes of interdiction. Where the water is allowed to settle it will take longer to dissolve this cumulative build up.

Question: Will it clean all the tube environment from calcium/aragonite deposits in the long term?

You wrote that the longest distance after the unit should not go over 300 feet, otherwise the structure of water gets lost again - does this happen suddenly or in a falling curve- like 100 feet = 95% structured, 200 feet 80 % structured, 300 feed 30% structured?

Answer: After 300 linear feet the Structuring will fall off. However, if the water is open to Nature you will experience an entrainment effect. If within the 300 feet there is an accumulation of stuff that utilizes the majority of "life force energy" initially produced, the results will be evident and structuring will only partially be available at the end of 300 feet. Hence the reason for the difference between a Shower, Under Sink and a Whole House unit structuring affect. Also I want reiterate here the Commercial unit is bigger, but unless you have a higher pressure and 2" or 1.5" of water flow, it will not give you more structuring. All of the Structured Water units are specifically designed. In the long run, more booster units in a long water line where the water is being utilized along the way, will serve one better than trying to do it with one large unit. The closer Structured Water is to the point of use the greater the benefit.

Where the Structured Water is moving it will clear calcium within minutes of interdiction. Where the water is allowed to settle it will take longer to dissolve this cumulative build up.

Question: I want to use your unit to structure distilled water that I have made, on the grounds that unlike the main domestic water supply, distilled water contains no pollutants to start with and once structured, could be expected to be even more effective at detoxification than polluted water that has been structured.

I only have a very low pressure pump however, to push the distilled water through the water structuring unit and do not know if the unit will work properly in this context.

Answer: Structuring distilled water will change its energy from hungry water to living water, water that knows what is good for life and what is not. Low pressure will still structure your water, just not as efficiently as under normal pressure. If you are drinking this distilled (and then structured) water I would recommend adding nutritional minerals to your water before drinking.

Question: How are the chemicals in the city water dissolved and then how are they eliminated from the device. I understand how it cleans the water pipes, say of calcium and must run the water till it is clear. I don't completely understand how the chemicals are eliminated by the water through the device.

Answer: Everything in the water is structured; gases go into the air, frequency memories are erased and the physical goes out your elimination system. You are a filter for all you eat. What part of an apple goes into your cells? Information; the same way a breatharian receives sustenance. Dr Edward Group has documented over 60,000 breatharians world wide.

Structured water, the truth of Nature, can only carry into the cells that which is good for life. All these elements ride on the outside of the water molecule in the form of memory and are instantly made available at the cellular level upon demand. Structured Water, instant hydration, at the cellular level attracts into itself that which is detritus to life such as heavy metals, disease, toxins, free radicals and all elements not part of ones original DNA or RNA. In other words the Truth of Nature cannot harm Nature. It is always a benefit without effort.

Question: I have someone who wants to know why their unit isn't changing the taste of the water like we said it would. They said it is helping their skin and hair but the water still tastes like chlorine.

Answer: Remember, if you have chlorine in your water and you structure it, chlorine gas is lighter than water and heavier than air. So after structuring and organizing, chlorine gas will rise to the surface of your glass of water so you may smell it and taste it. A solution would be to blow on the surface of the water or fill the container till it overflows. Depending on the amount of chlorine added to the source you may have to allow your water to set for a few minutes before consuming.

The other aspect of chlorine and any other previous contaminants within your source water prior to structuring will remain in a physical and vibratory state. These contaminates remain embedded in the residual calcium and aggregates in your pipe system until they are fully dissolved by the Structured Water.

Question: Also they want to know if the water stays structured when they cook with it (boil). Like when they boil potatoes will the water stay structured and so they don't have to worry about fluoride going into the potatoes and then into their system unstructured?

Answer: Structured Water remains so through boiling and cannot carry with it anything detrimental to life. Just blow on the top of your glass and it will mostly be gone. Also you can treat it as a fine wine and let it breath.

Question: I would like more detail. My biggest question/concern is that you are running water thru PVC as opposed to copper or stainless or glass. I would appreciate more info on materials and also more details on how it works.

Answer: When water is in the first turn of the structuring event it is erasing all the memories of its interactive experience with humanity. When water structuring is in the bliss of freedom, it doesn't regard, see, or feel the PVC that is promoting this new found experience of freedom. However, when Structured Water reaches the end of the structuring event it is armed with a full complement of attributes to fulfill its destiny. Structured waters destiny is to protect humanity, to the fullest extent within its field of influence, from all energies detrimental to life. The first challenge it will face in its new found freedom is the brass fitting it finds upon its exit from the structuring unit. Brass is carcinogenic and Structured Waters immediate solution is to shield the future water upon exit from the unit from this hazard to life. The perspectives Structured Water has to face to fulfill its destiny are too numerous to go into at this time.

Structuring Water through metals such as steel or copper reduces the maximum potential of the structuring event. Structuring through glass? People can't even handle plastic without breakage. My ultimate solution will be in a form of technology not yet available to surface dwellers but I know of it and we will implement it in time.

Question: I have someone whose well water is registering about a 4.5 pH. She ordered a Kangen machine, but the highest pH it will make is about 6.8-7. If we put a restructuring device of yours on the whole house, it would change the vibration of the water going in, but it wouldn't show up chemically. Is that correct?

Answer: YES. A Kangen machine does not have a way to discharge the materials and energies in the water so when you do a chemical test on its output, what do you get? Structuring the water before using a Kangen machine will make it more efficient.

Well water being subjected to no contact with the outer world is potentially a wonderful thing but remember we are seeking a most perfect water. That being said; Nature's view would be balance, balance, balance. Ground water is incomplete. It does need to have access with air to be more close to that balance. Air provides access to a property of water, air and balance not recognized by many, if any. Air provides Noble Gases, an essential aspect of the life giving properties of water. This is one more of the supreme attributes of Structured Water. Structured Water brings about this attribute instantaneously, however, even it for its absolute perfection, requires contact with air.

Question: If I test the water coming from one of your machines, how will it perform using a test for chlorine and/or fluoride as in this test kit?

Answer: More than likely there will be no difference before and after because you will be using conventional chemistry. Chemistry looks at the physical presence of materials; what is in the water is still in the water. However when the water is structured these materials are organized, Structured, their electromagnetic – chemical structure is changed. Chemistry will not see the difference. We are talking about physics. To see the change and measure this you need an Infrared Mass spectroscopy unit. Then the structure can be viewed down to the nano or molecular level.

I am currently associated with an organization that is in agreement to establish a most modern scientific laboratory for me to prove my knowledge of water and beyond.

Question: I have someone who wants to order an under the sink unit but they want to put it on after their reverse osmosis system. After looking at my parents RO system it doesn't look possible because of the little tubing that attaches it to the separate water spout on top of the sink. And the pressure isn't as high after it goes through the system.

1. Is it possible to attach it after the Reverse Osmosis system?

2. If not, what would happen to the structured water if it went through the Reverse Osmosis if they put it on before it?

Answer: Either way it works to the fullest extent of its field of influence. If placed before RO it erases memory and structures all materials making the RO more efficient. If placed after RO it erases the memory. To me RO is a deception. It removes the stuff from the water. But the memory, the vibrations in the water, go forward. It's the memory that kills you. I ask this question; when you eat an apple, what part of that apple goes into your cells? Answer; the vibrations of all that is good for life.

Question: So, with the filter on the unit will it still be able to structure the water?

Answer: YES. If you put the Structured Water unit on before the filter the filter will last longer but may reduce your ph by 1 point. Either way the water's attributes will be maximized to the fullest extent of the water's influence.

Question: For years we had a whole-house carbon filter on the main so that we could tolerate the water. We removed the filter before installing the Water Restructuring Unit. It's been a few weeks and drinking the water is intolerable. We tested the water today and got the following readings: Chlorine 5.2 PH 8.2

I cannot drink the water unless I put lots of lemon juice in it and I can still smell the chlorine. I realize you said that if we put the carbon filter back on the line it will deplete the hydrogen in the water; but I can't figure out how to "sample" the structured water to potential customers without them turning their noses up at the chlorine. If we put the filter back on the line we would put it before your unit.

Answer: Put your filter back on. All it will do is potentially reduce your ph by one point leaving you with ph of 7.2 or so. Putting it before or after (your choice).

Question: I have a house unit and am noticing more water softness which would make me assume it would also be removing lime deposits in my pipes….however, after a week, I have not seen any increase in pressure/volume in my hot water side and when I evicted 2 gal. of water from my hot water heater tank I didn't see anything in terms of lime, just clear water?? Also, I had thought the taste would reflect a loss of chlorine in it which it has not, so my questions are why or why not?

Answer: There are many more associates in this Structured Water journey now that embrace what I am about to write in response to your questions. It isn't easy to phrase this answer when one has not had an ample experience of the adjustment that is already permeated within you but regardless it is time to place this truth of Nature up for discussion.

There exists a lot of extenuating circumstance in water's world – our World. The unique advantage we have is manifesting all that we focus on. So I say to you, be aware of the thoughts you think and words you speak when in the presence of Structured Water and you are hydrated. What you focus on expands exponentially.

When water is in the structuring event so are all the materials and memories that are present in the water. Structure means organization. Since we can see the change and organization of calcium and feel the change on our skin and see the change in our plants and animals; why can we not believe this change in organization exists in all the other properties of the water when structuring occurs. We are all standing on the threshold of a new paradigm. It is our choice to step forward and Structured Water is there to aid us in our journey.

Question: Would a person put a unit (question on which one) on a pool if it was already filled? or would one just add some structured water? I remember your saying in sun it starts to turn back in 7-10 days, so in my thinking it seems it would be best on a pool if the structured water keeps going through the water structuring device. What would be the best way?

Answer: Use a unit that is in line with the pump insuring constant maximum structuring and oxygenation of the water.

Question: On our water, it seemed that the water when boiled on stove was clear and now we are getting a little whitish color on sides of pan again. Nothing like before the unit was installed though. I was wondering if this is still possibly sediment coming from pipes, or faucet? Or is it possible it may never be totally clear when we boil water due to the hardness? I assume, regardless, it shouldn't hurt us since it should still be filtered out of us when we drink it?

Answer: This condition is probably a combination of both and yes it will just pass through you.

Question: What about setting bowls of structured water around in areas of the home? The "stuffy air" of apartments can be a problem, especially in winter. I would also think, with gem elixers also in the water, some amazing help could be felt. Setting intentions, and even Feng Shui could make that a wonderful experiment.

Answer: Remember it's all about energy. When YOU set an intention, either vocally or silently, you will potentially manifest this. Be in the moment. The words you speak and the thoughts you think are forming your Destiny.

Question: The chlorine smell and taste were in the water container even 1 day later in the fridge. Does the unit need to be run several times before the smell and taste go away? It wasn't coming from the unit, I smelled it over 1 hour later in the container I put the water in and the taste was there too. Please advise if I may have done something wrong?

Answer: Influences of all the materials that were in your water before structuring are locked in the residual calcium and aggregates within your existing water system. As structured Water moves through, it will eventually dissolve these aggregates and their lodged influences. This condition is similar to the human body; if we have gallstones or kidney stones these formations hold the memory of all the diseases in our system. We may eliminate the diseases but if we don't simultaneously eliminate these stones within a short period, all our previous diseases reappear. In other words give it a little time. In my installation instructions I relate the possibility it may take a month or so.

Question: My daughter lives in a community in NH that has such high levels of arsenic in their city water that they can't drink it. She wants to purchase a house unit and is wondering if it would "remove" the arsenic and make the water safe to drink. Your thoughts, please.

Answer: Yes, it will make the water safe to drink. The water and everything in it is Structured, molecularly changed.

Question: When someone first starts drinking or showering in the water are there any detox reactions one has to be careful of as there are with the ionizer machines made by companies like Kangen? My son recently had surgery and I want to make sure if I install this on the kitchen sink or the bathroom shower it won't cause any problems for him.

Answer: Structured Water is Natures perfectly balanced Hydration. All of its attributes work in harmony to bring about a smooth transition back to perfect health and well-being. This is in effect the mandate of Structured Water to enhance and protect mankind. If you wish a more in depth explanation don't hesitate to ask.

There are systems out there that tout these same attributes, but only provide one. When this occurs, balance is lost and man loses.

Question: Your Structured Water Home Unit was installed in our home here in Sarasota, Florida by a licensed plumber on June 26, nine days ago. Since then our tap water has consistently tested acidic, 6.4 or below, rather than the alkaline pH of 7.0 – 7.5 claimed in its performance specifications.

Answer: No the unit is not defective. Do you have a carbon filter in line? If so, carbon reduces hydrogen approximately one point, 7.5 down to 6.5. Another carbon bonding effect is the buildup of calcium in your pipes and appliances, and until these conditions have been eliminated, the hydrogen content of your water may be compromised. Regardless of this temporary reduction in hydrogen, your newly Structured Water is contributing virtually hundreds of additional attributes into you and your environment. Don't focus on what is not. Allow what Structured Water is opening up in your presence.

Question: I received my shower system yesterday and installed it. I am very pleased with it. I do have a question. I am filling containers from the shower of water that I will drink. The water still tastes like tap water. I changed the shower head.

Is it okay to still filter the water through a Brita filter? Does this affect the quality of the water and defeat the structured water system?

Answer: You can filter it, RO it, distill it, freeze it, boil it and it will not lose its life force energy.

Question: Have you tested things such as the ORP, TDS, pH, etc... for this water? Does it really take out all chlorine, chloramine, and heavy metals?

Answer: All tests have been done and every source may be different. The water is Structured Water and all within it is also structured. The elements and conditions are not removed they are structured (molecularly changed – just as a diamond and coal are the same substance but they are different structurally).

Question: I have extremely hard well water that ruins clothes and turns the insides of washing machines orange. We have a water softener to deal with the problem. How would it work with a system like mine?

Answer: Structured Water will make your water soft without your current softener but you can add this to your system and make the water healthier for your body. If you place the unit before your softener it will make the softener more efficient or after it will add in healthy water. After installation you may try your water with your softener turned off.

Structured Water Natures way is an active sacred geometric form. Drinking and bathing with this sacred water will potentially bring your whole being into alignment.

Question: What is the difference in the water which runs thru the shower unit compared with the under the sink unit??? There is a difference in size of the units, so I am assuming the water with the kitchen unit is of a higher vibration. Do you have a sense of how much more??????

Answer: The Under Sink unit has a 4% increase in Bio-Photon energy over the Shower; the Home unit has a 13% increase in Bio-Photon energy over the Shower unit. The Shower unit's water is direct contact, no loss, the Under Sink water has to deal with stuff and that stuff is energy consuming.

Question: I am interested in the Home Unit. Does this have the capacity to provide structured water to an outdoor swimming pool in an enclosed patio? If so, would this make routine pool maintenance that now treats the water by adding chlorine, etc. unnecessary?

Answer: Structured Water will reduce the need for chemicals and this will be dependent on the circulation of your pool. Structured water substantially increases the stable oxygen and bio-Photon content of the pool water therefore increasing aerobic bacteria (good bacteria) and decreasing anaerobic bacteria (bad bacteria). The real neat aspect of Structured Water in a swimming pool is it knows what is good for life and what is not. When you are in your pool you will feel very energized and only that which is good for you will enter into your cells. The truly unique thing about this technologically advanced Structured Water system is it is unconditionally guaranteed. How can you go wrong?

Question: Would it be possible for someone to relate to me the difference, if any, in how free radicals are neutralized?

One last question. I have learned much about my drinking water through enagic and the kangen water system of ionized water. They measure an important factor called oxidation reduction potential (ORP) or the ability to share negative electrons to neutralize positive free radicals.

Answer: ORP is a very important measurement for ionized water (electrocuted water). However Structured Water is Natures balance water that is perfectly balanced with your body. It contains a substantial amount of free stable oxygen that increases necessary oxygen to all your bodily functions. pH and ORP are the two main factors with Kangen water.

Structured Water is Natures perfection of life giving elements that empower mankind to be free and fulfill their own destiny Structured water has the power to know what is good for life and what is not. As this water passes through your body it can only carry with it that which is good for life and as it passes through your cells it will assimilate within itself all that is detrimental to life (this includes free radicals).

Question: Thank you very much for the detailed information. I have been making/using/studying various water structuring devices and methods for some years now and am strongly thinking of buying your garden unit or perhaps a whole-house one. When I have time, I structure water for plants using a magnet-vortex connector between two 2 soda bottles, and it works really well! A form of bio-dynamics I guess?

Anyway, I need your advice before I decide which unit to buy: We have a whole-house Wellness water filter that conditions and structures all the water inside the house. The water outside for the garden does not go through the Wellness filter. Clearly, the plants would benefit from structured water, which could be accomplished with the garden unit; but would the Wellness filter undo (or perhaps enhance?) what the whole-house unit would do?

With great appreciation for your work, and looking forward to drinking your water out of my garden hose if not the kitchen sink—

Answer: The whole house Structured Water unit will enhance all equipment and life in the waters path, plus the added enhancement of entrainment on that which is within its field of influence. And if you can place it in your source water line before your hose outlets it will also significantly enhance the growth, production, longevity and life force energy (bio-photons) of everything in the Structured Water's path. Remember the 300 foot rule, so more units strategically placed will not only improve your lives but also your environment and draw unto you and yours benefits yet unseen.

Question: Do you have an opinion on how this water compares to freshly harvested spring water straight from Mother Earth that I go get myself?

Answer: As to your question about spring water, this is a difficult question to answer. The best answer I can give is for you to exercise your own intuition. Your body knows what is good for you and the more you are in tune with Nature, Structured water, the more power you have over your own environment. Know thy self, have dominion. We could have an interesting conversation with this and beyond.

Question: The couple I am talking to says to tell you they are stubborn and need to know, if the contaminates in the water are not filtered, is the "water Safe to drink"?

Answer: The water is safe but if they choose for it or anything else not to be so, then "what you seek you shall find." They also can add a filter. I don't know what else I can give you or them. Structured Water is an act of God, an aid for mankind to become.

Question: I still don't understand what happens with the sediment and minerals in the water if nothing is removed and it's not filtered in some way. Presumably one drinks those and they go on through the body and are expelled with the other sludge removed from the organs and tissues, etc.?

Answer: So what goes into your cells when you eat an apple? It's the music, the vibrations of the minerals and vitamins. Everything physical goes out your elimination system. When water is structured, the memory of that which is detrimental to life, is erased and the good elements that enhance life are carried forward and made available at the cellular level. The thing to remember is ALL that passes through the Structured Water unit is changed at the molecular level. In this structuring event everything is organized and coherent. When you get your Structured Water unit installed, you will have much more to add to this brief explanation. One of the first things you will notice of your surroundings is calcium buildup falls away and everything is sparkling clean, as it will also be within you. However we do have free choice, but I wonder about that too, because as the memory of past traumas within are erased, so are the scars and the limp.

So am I right? After your experience with Structured Water, you tell me. Remember also, there are many professed sources of Structured Water out there, but what I am offering through Ultimate Water is Natures perfect, balanced and energized water without moving parts, magnets, chemicals, salts or electronic enhancements. My simple Structured Water unit has a lifetime unconditional warranty. And guess what? This is just the beginning. There is more to come. Everyone joining with me in bringing forth the Truth of Structured Water is investing, as a partner, in enhancing and enlivening the Truth of Nature, of which we are a significant part. It's all a symbiotic relationship; fix one and then on to the next journey.

Question: How does your under sink unit compare to ionizers such as the Tyent water ionizer?

Answer: Ionized water is best described as electrocuted water (water that is pulled apart by electricity). If you refer back to the previous question regarding what is absorbed into the cells of the body (the music and vibrations), I personally would not want to absorb the chaotic energy of ionized water. It doesn't feel right to me. However, we are all on our own individual journey and we all have free will.

Question: Since water has memory, is reverse osmosis water still harmful even after filtering?

Answer*:*

Not as harmful if you add minerals. The Bio-Photon level, pH, viscosity, density, and life force energies I have not looked at, but the memory issue, I know, is more correct.

Question: Where can I get more information about structured water?

Answer: Please see the web site section on videos, articles and websites on Structured Water and related information.

Question: Where do the contaminates go?

Answer: The simplicity of these Structured Water units structure all that is within the water. Therefore, through structuring, not only is the water changed but also the materials within it go through an electro-chemical realignment. This is similar to the perspective of a lump of coal and a diamond having identical properties, the only difference is structure. Structured water hydrates life. The materials not beneficial to life go through your body as a discharge of refuge.

Structured Water, the truth of Nature, can only carry forth into life elements beneficial to life.

Question: I recently obtained a garden unit for home and garden use…however I discovered that the unit doesn't remove the minerals from the tap water thereby making the water undrinkable…my solution is to obtain water from Kinetico Water and run their water through your unit. I will use a height difference of 3-4 ft when running the K. water through the filter….is this enough pressure to activate your device? Is there a minimum pressure requirement for the unit to work?

Answer: These Structured Water units are not designed to remove minerals, they structure the minerals. An example of structuring is; a lump of coal and a diamond have identically the same materials, the only difference is structure. When calcium is structured, it no longer has the electro-chemical ability to adhere to itself, much less what it comes in contact with. Therefore, all that will remain is a powdered calcium which will pass through you as roughage. For the Garden unit to effectively Structure Water any distance will work, however, the greater the pressure, the greater the efficiency. Thirty pounds per square inch (PSI) is an average pressure. If less than that, structuring will still be effective. An optimum pressure is fifty PSI +. In the near future I will have the scientific equipment to prove exactly at what pressure each device works best at, and at what level, if any, it is no longer beneficial.

Question: Also the manager at Kinetico says the mineral content of their water is 10-30 ppm….do I need to add minerals for your device to work at optimum levels?

Answer: I would add a liquid monatomic mineral supplement to any water. There are very few waters on this planet that contain all the minerals essential to life and if you're going to add minerals, use monatomic. It's instantaneous just like the water.

Question: My parents live in a single family home, and I suggested they get a whole house unit. The website I was on recommends the Commercial for this case. Can you please tell me if this is okay?

Answer: The only reason you would need a Commercial unit for a home is if the water line flow coming into the home is greater than one inch, which is the internal diameter of the pipe it's to be installed on. For the majority of home applications the smaller, less expensive whole House Structured Water units are sufficient for most water conditions.

Question: What is the difference between the Home Unit and the Home Ultimate unit? Is the Home Ultimate unit available yet?

Answer: The Home Ultimate Water unit cleans and removes the excess materials released when the memory of the water is erased. The Ultimate is more for that discerning individual that expects perfection and is willing to pay for it. It is not yet available.

Question: I have a friend who wants to use hexagonal water for a soil amendment product we are going to be manufacturing. Does the structured water unit create hexagonal water?

Answer: Yes it does create hexagonal water (a natural balance ~ fact of Nature). Structured Water is Natures balance.

Question: Could you refresh my memory as to the volume and pressure of water the Ultimate unit is capable of, as well as type of filter (ie micron rec.) and how particulate separation, monthly service/maintenance schedule, etc. with any other info specifications for adaptation to irrigation systems.

Answer: The Ultimate unit will be a one inch in/out flow capable of 100 psi + if needed. We usually place a pressure regulator to approximately 50 psi on them for residential use.

There is no filter. It is the dynamic effect of the water itself that allows the removal of all materials heavier than water to be discharged along with about 1/8 to ¼ inch flow depending upon the contaminates in the water. There is no maintenance, no filter, no moving parts and no electricity for Ultimate units used on a well. The best place for this discharge on a well unit is to place it back down into the reservoir at the well head. This will facilitate the ground waters to become less contaminated.

For units that will be used in an environment with constant water pressure there needs to be an electronic control to detect water flow and simultaneously open a valve to allow for the discharge. The discharge from this unit can be used for many applications including irrigation of vegetation such as trees, shrubs or down the drain, which enhances drainage water or your septic tank.

These units are not available as of yet.

Question: I have a question about metal toxicity such as aluminum, mercury, arsenic in water......what do the filters do with that? or is it handled with the filters?

Answer: Structured Water has been given many attributes of the balance of Nature, but the elements within the water are also dynamically charged to a neutral state. These potentially toxic materials are made inert through structuring. Also Structured Water cannot carry with it anything other than that which is good for life into a living cell. All other materials or elements go out the elimination system.

Question: I have been testing the pH with an old pH roll of paper. It is only showing a pH of about 6. Why do you think that would be the case? Any ideas so I can raise my level of knowledge and confidence as I teach others about this.

Answer: Hydrogen is absorbed by carbon so if you have a carbon filter in your system it will reduce your hydrogen level approximately one point. So what is the pH reading before the Structuring unit? Other things that detour pH are forms of carbon which may be aggregates built up in the existing system or a Reverse Osmosis system or some other conditioning system. In other words the most perfect water to structure would be water out of nature. Everything man made in between water and life is detrimental to life. These Structuring Water units will, to the best of their ability, protect man from his own devices and bring about balance within its presence, regardless of intervention, even if you can't see it or prove it.

Question: I also have someone wondering if they could use the structured water unit on their rain harvesting system. What do you think?

Answer: Absolutely! It will make rain water more perfect and if you need more specifics ask.

Installation and Placement

Question: I just purchased an under sink unit from you and I'm trying to figure out the best way to install it. I have an under sink Multi pure (charcoal) filter unit with a sink side faucet. If I attach the structured water unit before the filter, it will have the best and most consistent faucet delivery, as the water to the filter is always pressurized. Will that set up deliver the desired structured water? or do I need to hook it up directly to the above sink faucet?

Answer: Hook it up where it fits best for you. Regardless of where it is placed, you will receive Structured Waters' multitudes of benefits.

Question: We are purchasing another home that has a well. We will be having the water tested, but I understand that there is currently a filter and water softener installed. Where do I install your unit? Before or after the filter and softener? Is it possible for this unit to eventually replace these other units or do they perform a different function?

Answer: Placement of your Structured Water unit may be before all other water conditioners, it will just make them more efficient, or after these systems. Regardless, structuring will improve your health and well-being. If you have a carbon filter after the Structured Water unit it will potentially decrease the ph about one point, 7.5 down to 6.5. Additionally, any calcium build up in conditioners and pipes will also cause a potential decrease in pH (hydrogen).

I suggest placement be such that hose bibs and all other water outlets have the benefit of Structured Water. It will change your world. Remember the 300 foot rule; Structured Water is only effective for 300 linear feet, after which it becomes dead under pressure (moving water). However if the water lines have Structured Water in them and water flow is terminated (shut off) then we have a condition called entrainment and all the waters connected will be entrained and therefore Structured (a Truth of Nature).

Most people turn off their water softeners and conditioners because Structured Water is soft like rain water (another Truth of Nature). Know that in time everything in your home and surroundings will eventually be in tune (harmony) with Nature. I have a friend who likes to demonstrate the differences between Structured Water and tap water. He has to go to his neighbors to get chlorinated city water for his demonstrations, but finds when he brings it home, it too, is structured.

Question: I have a 2300 square foot house, one story, "L" shaped. It has been added onto twice and I'm not really sure how the pipes run. There are three full baths, one half and one quarter. There are two water heaters. I would like something to take care of the house and the sprinklers. Would one whole house unit do this?

Answer: The Whole House unit will serve you very well.

Question: I will install the home unit at the point where the waterline enters my home so everything with be using structured water. This includes the landscaping and fish pond (500 gallons) which draw their water from connections inside the house. This means that a total of about 30,000-50,000 gallons of water a month will be passing through the structuring unit and all the way through my home. The house is tightly sealed/ weatherproofed for efficiency to prevent loss of heat or cooling. If I understand correctly, the water structuring system will be converting the chlorine in the 40,000 gallons of water into a chlorine gas which will dissipate through the highest point in my home's water line. The high points in this case would be the faucets and shower heads. I am wondering if this quantity of toxic chlorine gasses and possible other vaporized contaminants, constantly released into the sealed environment of my home each day will be a health concern? If not, could you explain please. Is the chlorine gas toxic?

Answer: It is structured along with the water, and in my view, this places these things in a sphere of no harm, however, to scientifically prove this knowing of mine an Infrared Mass Spectrometer will be required to show definitely what is in the air and the percentage of that element. There are many more considerations here. Is it better to ingest these toxins or to release them? Why are they present in your life? Is it not for us to get beyond this view of resistance?

Back to what I know Structured Water will do. To the fullest extent of its' ability (in its field of influence) it will protect you and yours from all things detrimental to life by pulling these toxins into itself if there are toxins after Structuring.

Question: Most of our pipe is 1-1/4" and I was planning on bushing down the two units I have. Does this minimize performance in any way?

Answer: You can bush down the Commercial units and they will do just fine.

Question: I have a circulating pump on the hot water line in my home which keeps the hot water moving all the time. This allows hot water to be waiting at the faucet in the bathrooms which are a long distance from the hot water tank and therefore saves running the water while it "warms up" for a shower. Will this pump or continual hot water movement negatively impact the structured water? Similarly, will the circulating pump and constant water movement in the fish pond damage the structuring of the water?

Answer: If your water is constantly circulating without a source of freshly structured water within the system, it will become dead after moving 300 feet under pressure. The solution is to install another house unit on the circulating line so it is freshly structured each time it passes through. The fish pond would be best served by having a structuring device somewhere in line with the pump unless freshly structured water is coming from another source.

Question: What if I live in an apt complex?

Answer: For an apartment application a Shower unit will work anywhere and an Under Sink is applicable if your complex is ok with it. They are both easy to install.

Question: I received your Under Sink device. Can you advise me how to attach? or can I just let it sit on something? In other words, can it be free-standing (hanging)?

Answer: It can hang free or you can go to a hardware store and buy a 2 inch wall bracket in the electrical department for securing a 2 inch PVC pipe stand for electrical installations.

Question: I have yet to notice any difference in the water quality as of yet. Do you recommend any specific test or demonstration to potential customers? I love the idea of your product but still need some convincing of its effectiveness.

Answer: I have sent testimonials and information I can't think of any more than to try muscle testing or dowsing.

Portability and Storage of Structured Water

Question: What is the best container to store water in?

Answer: When you are in a place of needing to fill containers with Structured Water for later use; there are several considerations. It would be easier for me to answer this question on the phone, but there are others who also have a need to know this answer with the availability to reference the answer over and over. When water is structured it will be constantly incorporating its mandate to protect life. Structured Water will to the fullest extent of its ability assimilate into itself all energies detrimental to life (to include disharmony, stress, toxins, hydrocarbons, elements that detour life just to name a few). As Structured Water pulls these elements within it; it is assimilating memory. Memory is an attribute of water that potentially takes it back to whence it came, convoluted. The only way to correct this condition is for water to return back to its natural origin and then reemerge to again blossom into its freedom to do what it is meant accomplish. Our structured water devices accomplish this.

Question: Does the water prefer glass to plastic containers?

Answer: No. However we have to be practical. Everything man made is detrimental to life.

Question: What is the duration of live water in stored containers? 30-60 days in direct sunlight.... how about overcast and evenings – dark? Since we really don't "know" this is a sincere if foolish-sounding question.

Answer: The duration Structured Water remains structured depends upon its surroundings in the moment. Direct sunlight 7 to ten days but if it is indoors or covered it will stay structured for a time depending on its surroundings. If the energy in its field of influence is detrimental to life, it will correct this energy to the fullest extent of its ability and once saturated will fall back. If the energy is enlivening and life giving it will last a very long time.

Question: Do any of these - heating, cooking, refrigerating, alter water's qualities?

Answer: No!

Question: If water's in a glass container, does a plastic lid alter it? how about a metal lid?

Answer: Structured Water will to the best of its ability correct all elements detrimental to life in its field of influence; this statement includes these things plus everything man made.

Question: Is it o.k. to carry this water in a stainless steel thermos when going out? and carrying in car?

Answer: Yes. But it is not perfect either.

Question: Where does one find sodium bentonite clay containers?

Answer: I have not looked for them. As I proceed through my journey they will be produced and available to all who ask.

Question: Lacking the cobalt glass and/or bentonite containers; can you suggest some suitable shielding material one can wrap the container in that will help preserve this water? There is a shielding film that Ormus producers keep their products in and mail them in. It sort of resembles very thin shiny aluminum but it isn't and I can't at all recall now what it's called. You will no doubt know this. Will this be an o.k. material to wrap water container in?

Answer: In my view Structured Water is meant to be free so I wouldn't be much help.

Question: My question is, it looks like the only devices for sale are ones that must be hooked up to the piping for the sink/faucet, shower faucet, etc. I don't drink tap water, currently I just buy bottled spring water like Deer Park. I would like to use your device to structure my bottled water. Do you have stand alone device that would do this? Or will one of the faucet type devices on the website work if I just kept it on the counter and poured my bottled water through it into an empty container?

Answer: There are people doing exactly what you seek just pouring their water through the unit. It does work, however, the more pressure you have the more the efficiency you will potentially get. I am working to produce a portable unit you can carry with you.

Question: I talked to a friend who I told the unit about, and she said that the water from the unit does not stay structured indefinitely. Was she mistaken, or is this true? I was under the impression that once the water is structured, as long as it doesn't travel through a long length of straight pipe, it stays structured. I have been filling up a jug from my shower unit every morning to drink during the day assuming that it stayed structured. Would you mind clarifying this for me?

Answer: Structuring; lasts under pressure only 300 feet of straight pipe. In direct sun light – seven to ten days. Indoors in an environment of calm without stress and a natural surrounding – up to 45 days plus. In a plastic container in your car (not in direct sun light) – up to thirty days.

However, imagine structured water running in a straight pipe under pressure ten miles long. A valve at the other end is shut off. When that valve is shut off, all the water in the pipe is instantly structured. The term for the event is entrainment. Structured water placed in the presence of any other water will cause it, also, to be structured by entrainment.

Consciousness and Water

Question: Q&A response to the persistent requests for authoritative documentation regarding the effects of Structured Water.

Answer: The scientific community around the world abounds with various research, findings, articles and analysis of water structure, its enhancement, its quality and the immense value of its energetic effects on living things. For those of you requesting more info, more answers about the effects of Structured Water on plants, animals, bacteria, virus, and other microbial life forms as well as analytical observations of water's energetic effects on molecular structures, chemical reactions, enzymes and mineral substances in "non living" components of the world around us, I can only say yes, the data is immense. It is overwhelming but equally quite incomprehensible.

Despite the countless fortunes being spent in furthering scientific understanding of water and its energetic structure, the most effective and greatest analyzer remains the human mind and body. Our senses are tens of thousand times more sensitive than the most expensive and elaborate analyzer. Despite the great advancements in scientific research, the analysis drawn from our basic human senses are what the worlds fortunes most rely. Personal experience remains the truest test and the highest value is placed on that experience. The analysis of our worlds' oldest and largest industries (i.e.) Medical, Food, Cosmetics, wine and beer depend almost exclusively on the final word of personal experience, personal observation, person taste, personal touch. Our health and the health of world population and industry depend on our five senses (our personal analyzer) and it is to this ultimate scrutiny we submit our Structured Water Devices.

We will continue to test, gather data, and expand our understandings and applications. We will continue gathering collaborations with the worlds' top scientific minds and expand existing studies and related research to add to our own in an effort to help meet the needs of those wishing to use, promote and expand the implementation of these remarkable life enhancing, world changing devices, however, much of this material (both officially published and non-published research data) is and will remain highly complex and in many if not most cases make little meaningful sense to anyone outside these scientific fields of inquiry.

So here in the end as in all new beginnings it is you who must determine what is good for you. It is you we most trustfully rely. It is your experience, your insight, your personal experience and results we most implore. We and all those using and researching these devices know their value. We see the results but it is you who most ultimately determine its value. The only true failure is to fail to try, to fail to inquire, explore. What is of most value for you can truly be best determined by you. We can offer our experience and findings but you are your own best resource, best advisor and best personal counsel for what is good, healthy and beneficial for you. For more information on these units you may stay tuned to our websites, blogs and newsletters but, for the surest truth, the best testimonial will be your own. Don't wait, order one today, risk free, fully guaranteed and lovingly offered in exchange for your testing and experience which will always remain our most valued commodity.

Comment: Wonderful advice. Thank you. It was hard for me growing up. I did things people weren't suppose to do and it got me into lots of trouble. For many, many years I've been shut down. I just shut the door to it all. I've been a work in progress, finding my way back to myself. I'm sure that's why I developed the cancer. It was my wake-up call.

Comment: You are so wise. As you now know we are all here to participate. No putting your head in the sand. No wonder it has taken so long for humanity to get on with it, you weren't present. So that's not going to happen again, right?

Question: Maybe you could explain something to me. Years ago a friend came to visit me from Arizona. Before she left, she gave me a really nice turquoise ring with a oval stone. She told me before wearing it to take my pendulum and dowse the positive end and wear the positive end up towards my heart. I took my pendulum and lo and behold the ring had a positive side and a negative side. For some reason I took the ring and placed it in some water I had charged with my hands. I left it in there a couple of minutes, took it out and dowsed it before putting it on my finger. I dowsed and re-dowsed because BOTH sides of the ring were now positive according to my pendulum. I was told by my friend that any object like a pen, pencil, piece of pipe etc. will have a neg. and a pos. end, and my pendulum verified it. If I placed a pen or pencil in my charged water, once again both ends would be positive. I found out I just had to hold something and it changed. I have a feeling your units probably do the same thing. If you hold a pendulum over the palms of your hands, you should have one hand pos. and one neg. I have 2 positives. I had a person tell me I was a mono-pole whatever the

heck that is, if anything. I thought if anyone knew something about this, you would.
p.s. I love the concept of drinking our dreams!!

Answer: What a beautiful expression of knowing one's own power. It's all energy. We do have the power to bring it into our view. Our image. Congratulations on demonstrating this to yourself and sharing with me. Now take this knowing to other aspects of your life and be in joy.

Question: There is a retired chemist/engineer who comes to the Vipassana center between courses to take care of stuff and he is really sweet but he thinks that Structured Water is psuedo science. He said there is no real science that explains it. He says the only thing that makes water change its properties are the minerals or chemicals you add to it or take away from it. So he doesn't see how anything but an actual filter would make water healthier. He also believes that the crystal pictures that Masuro Emoto takes are ice crystals not water in its soluble form. If you have any good info I could relay to people like this that would be nice. If not, that is okay as well.

Answer: Believe me, a Chemist or Engineer has little or no concept of Physics. I would just let it go until we have proof that he could accept, but I am not sure that you will ever convince an educated man that may be unwilling to go beyond his envelope, his ego. That's possibly why he is there. I don't think it is our place to change people. The only way that can happen is for them to change from within.

Health Issues and Water

Question: I was wondering if you have come up with any studies on Giardia. I have someone interested in the unit who has a well and wanted to know if the Home Unit will protect them from Giardia.

Answer: See the word anaerobes (anaerobic) in the description. Structured water enhances aerobic bacteria and eliminates anaerobic bacteria. How does it do that? Well the answer is oxygen. Lots of free stable oxygen. This is an automatic result of Structured Water's balance of Nature. Again, I say Structured water cannot enhance elements detrimental to life and this statement is inclusive of diseases. Bodies of surface water, standing water, water in and around cooling systems, water that is used over and over is dead water; water void of free stable oxygen, void of life force energy and overburdened with memory.

The answer to your question is yes.

Giardia lamblia (synonymous with Lamblia intestinalis and Giardia duodenalis) is a flagellated protozoan parasite that colonises and reproduces in the small intestine, causing giardiasis. The giardia parasite attaches to the epithelium by a ventral adhesive disc, and reproduces via binary fission[1]. Giardiasis does not spread via the bloodstream, nor does it spread to other parts of the gastro-intestinal tract, but remains confined to the lumen of the small intestine[2]. Giardia trophozoites absorb their nutrients from the lumen of the small intestine, and are anaerobes. If the organism is split and stained, it has a very characteristic pattern that resembles a familiar "smiley face" symbol.

Question: Our well water in Moses Lake, WA is quite hard. Toilet rings and coffee makers go bad in a few months. One of us is now hurting from a bone spur. Will this take care of the problems? and will the house unit exempt us from needing the water softener? Is there a Guarantee?

Answer: The answer to all your questions is yes. Structured Water is soft water in a natural way and has healing properties too.

Question: My friend is a heart transplant recipient and I would like to give him some of the water and wonder what it would do to all the anti-rejection medication he is on. It would be wild if this water would restructure his heart DNA to have his body accept this heart and be totally off the medication. (That would have the Cleveland Clinic scratching their heads) On the other hand, I would not want to harm him if this would mess with his medications in a negative way. Any opinion?

Answer: There are many Clinics and Medicals professionals scratching their heads, but still not willing to cross the thresh-hold to the ease of balanced health and well-being Structured Water initiates this starting place to become. Structured Water instantly hydrates an absolute necessity for health and well-being. How could this harm? Structured water can only carry into the cellular level that which is beneficial for life. We could go on and on with this but I believe the question has been answered.

Question: A customer asked if the unit would destroy coliform bacteria. Although I understand that coliforms themselves are not the cause of sickness, their presence is used to indicate other pathogenic organisms of fecal origin; bacteria, viruses, etc. How would the unit "clean" these types of organisms?

Answer: This small unit cannot remove excessive contaminates, but it does have the capability to transform. To unequivocally say this is so in all cases needs further investigation. I do have an Ultimate unit that will discharge all materials heavier than water. Ultimate Structured Water units are currently being used to reclaim septic tank water. To say absolutely what the smaller unit will do with any type of excessive contaminates would require an on-site study. I am hoping to have such a mobile test system soon.

Question: I found the section where you talked about the ability of the structured water to remove harmful elements from the cells to be particularly fascinating. It made me wonder if you have received any feedback or have done any experiments with using the water to reduce or prevent hangovers from alcohol. I am not much of a drinker myself, but it seems like this could potentially be a good indicator of the power of the water if it could negate the deleterious effects of alcohol on the body by clearing it before it has the chance to do damage. Anyway, just a thought…

Answer: Alcohol and Structured Water; add one ounce of alcohol to eight ounces of Structured Water and your body will feel the effect of nine ounces of alcohol. It has to do with viscosity or water tension. Alcohol is approximately 28 Dynes and structured Water is approximately 43 Dynes. Our cells require that number to be below 46 Dynes to cross the cell wall. Drinking Structured Water will flush the alcohol effect more quickly. Also if your body is highly hydrated before drinking alcohol, by Structured Water, it will take an inordinate amount of alcohol to become intoxicated.

Protection From EMF's

Question: Does the water protect from EMF's; EM's; wifis? blackberry's and so on?

Answer: It will aid you to become more resilient and eventually help you to attain Dominion over all things not of you.

Question: Do you have devices you make, or can you suggest protective devices that really do protect (a person) that you know of?

Answer: Do you really want to live in a cage? If not, then read the above answer.

Entrainment

Question: I feel a little confused about entrainment. Do you mean because the water coming out of the device is contained and the structure is affecting that particular water, whatever is coming out is structured and regardless of how far the pipes go down in say your county or city, one is still getting optimal hydration?

Answer: Entrainment is a truth of Nature. When you walk into a room with others present you entrain upon them and they on you. Structured Water a perfection of Nature, entrains its energy onto all within its field of influence.

Question: Since this water entrains upon water and materials under its influence, how long does the influence hold on same?

Answer: It falls in the same guide lines as I have related of Structured Water in the answers above.

Question: I did watch the videos and saw where it would structure other water by being next to it. If I add a cup of structured water to a bucket of well water/tap water would the cup of water structure the whole bucket at that moment?

Answer: These Structured Water systems are specifically designed to fulfill an environment of health; well-being and efficiency for all in its path to the fullest extent of this waters ability so bigger is not necessarily better, however, more units strategically placed will extend this energy form indefinitely.

Regardless of what you pay for Structured Water, under pressure, it only structures water up to 300 feet. However, when there is Structured Water in a system and no water movement a new paradigm is present and that is a phenomenon called entrainment. Structured Water entrains upon all the water and materials in its field of influence. Look around; be aware, you are Structured Water.

Chapter 12. Testimonials

Testimonial for Clayton Nolte's Amazing Water Structuring Device by **Jacquelyn Aldana www.15minutemiracle.com**

When I first learned about Clayton Nolte's Water Structuring Device on Adam Abraham's "Talk for Food" Internet Radio Show, I very much wanted to believe it did everything he said it would…but, frankly, it sounded w-a-a-ay too good to be true.

But because Adam Abraham had proven to be a reliable source for exceptional products and services that "under-promise and over-deliver," I was inclined to believe this amazing device was the "real deal." At any rate, I felt compelled to investigate it further.

We had already invested over $8,000 in a sophisticated water filtration system for our well in 1989 that requires over $1,000 worth of maintenance every year. And in 1992, we invested in a $1,600 water ionizer (alkaline water machine) that required $50 worth of new filters every 4-6 months. I never realized how expensive it was just to maintain these devices.

We even installed a reverse osmosis unit under our kitchen sink thinking it would greatly enhance our health. We used it for several years until I found out it that RO water (reverse osmosis) is actually "dead water" that actually leaches minerals out of your body. Although RO systems remove contamination, they also remove all the calcium, potassium, and magnesium your body desperately needs for countless vital functions. I was also shocked to discover that distilled water, although very pure, was also doing the same thing. Minerals are vital to your cells, and when you drink water void of all minerals (RO and/or distilled water), your cells will pull the minerals they need out of your bones and tissues.

When I had a bone scan recently, it showed I was an extremely "high risk" for osteoporosis, so the last thing I need is anything pulling minerals out of my bones. Needless to say, the RO device was removed and we no longer drink distilled water. After investing over $9,600 in water enhancement systems and nearly $21,000 to maintain them, we still had a quality of water that was less than ideal even after spending a whopping $31,600! And up until a month ago, we were still searching for solutions.

If We Only Knew Then What We Know Now

The money we invested to purchase Clayton Nolte's Water Structuring Device turned out to provide the best return on investment we have ever made in anything…ever! Not only did it provide superior quality, life-enhancing "living water" from our kitchen sink, but from every water source inside and outside the entire house, the guest cottage, the studio, the stables, and every outbuilding on all three acres within 300' of the installation!

I honestly feel as though I'm drinking and bathing in "Liquid God." That's probably because Clayton Nolte's Structured Water produces bio-photons (light) and resonates at the same vibrational frequency as "Love" (528 HZ). And since "God is Love" and 528 HZ is known as the "Miracle Frequency," I was inspired to call Clayton's awesome invention **God's Miracle Water System**™.

Below are just some of the positive differences my husband (Mr. Skeptical) and I have experienced since installing **God's Miracle Water System**™ on August 1, 2009. Everything you read below was experienced within the first 30 days of installation.

Topic Personal Observations

Water Tastes Wetter and Better

We love the taste, feel, and consistency of **God's Miracle Water**™ because it has a silky, smooth quality unlike any water we've ever had. I love the idea that it's bringing IN the "good stuff" and taking OUT the "bad stuff" in my body every time I drink or bath in this naturally hydrating, pH balanced water.

Smooth, Clear, Beautiful Skin
(Moles, Skin Tags and Age Spots)

Within 3 days of bathing in **God's Miracle Water**™, two ugly skin tags fell right off my arms. I also noticed that a very large, dark, itchy, irritated mole on my back almost completely disappeared. I can barely see where it was now. The dark age spots all over my face, hands, and arms have begun to fade. If they keep fading at this rate, I expect to be "spotless" in a just a few months! When I had a professional facial recently, my esthetician was absolutely amazed at the condition and appearance of my skin. She said she only needed to use 1/3 of the products she normally used because my skin was so radiant, hydrated, and healthy looking.

Healthy, Silky, Shiny Hair

Every time I used to wash my hair, I noticed a substantial amount of hair in the drain. Now, when I wash my hair, I notice only a few (if any) strands clinging to the drain cover. Not only that, my hair is softer, shinier, and smoother than ever before…even when I don't use shampoo or conditioner!

Whiter Teeth and Healthier Gums

For several years, I have had bleeding gums, which is an indication of periodontal disease. Within 3 days of using **God's Miracle Water**™, I have had "zero bleeding" of my gums. Not only that, but my teeth look whiter.

Great Finger and Toenails

After a few weeks of bathing in and drinking **God's Miracle Water**™, my husband noticed that the fungus under his toenails was beginning to clear up! I, too, have noticed a big change in my fingernails. For the first time ever, they are long, strong and don't chip, peel, or break like they used to. Because my natural nails look so good, I don't even wear nail polish any more.

No More Junk Food Cravings

Since drinking **God's Miracle Water**™, I no longer crave foods and beverages that sabotage my health. I am naturally drawn to foods that nourish my body, and I now eat more sensibly than ever before.

Sparking Dishes – Sparking Dishwasher

Because we have excessive minerals in our well water, the dishes and glasses in our dishwasher always used to look dull and cloudy. This was downright embarrassing when we had company over for dinner. Since installing **God's Miracle Water System**™, our dishes and glasses sparkle and shine like someone hand polished them. Not only that, the inside of the dishwasher looks brand new!

Shiny Bathroom Sinks, Bathtub and Shower

The sinks, bathtub, shower, and toilet in our master bathroom are a rich, dark brown porcelain and fiberglass and have been quite a challenge to keep looking clean because of chalky mineral deposit buildup from our well water. I tried over 17 cleaning products (some of them quite toxic), and the only one that did any good at all was plain white vinegar…and even that didn't work that well. Since installing Clayton Nolte's **God's Miracle Water System**™ just one month ago, everything in the bathroom sparkles and shines…no more white, yukky stuff to dull the finish!

Indoor Plants Grew 30% Bigger in Just 3 Weeks

Within 3 weeks of watering our indoor plants with **God's Miracle Water**™, our plants have become so tall and wide that we have to transplant some of them into larger containers! Our living room is beginning to look like a jungle with furniture in it!

Outdoor Plants are Thriving

I have a rose bush that looked half dead that never produced a flower for the last 3 or 4 years. Within three days of watering it with **God's Miracle Water**™, a tiny rosebud appeared. The next day, I saw a beautiful crimson red rose in full blossom. The day after that, another bud appeared, followed by another beautiful floral display. I love it when things like this happen!

The same thing happened with a sorry-looking cactus plant that had never blossomed in the 8 years we've had it! I could hardly believe my eyes when I saw a beautiful bright orange flower with iridescent petals reaching toward the heavens in all their glory. I literally gasped in amazement!

We have a walnut tree that has looked almost dead for the past 3 years. Because my other plants responded so well to the structured water, I began to water this sad-looking tree with **God's Miracle Water**™ a few days ago. It may just be my imagination, but I am pretty sure the few leaves that are left on this tree are looking much more vital.

I have full faith that this precious tree will fully come back to life by Spring. After all, "With God (and God's Miracle Water), all things are possible." Since installing **God's Miracle Water System**™, every tree, plant, and scrub on our property is bigger and healthier looking than ever before. Our landscape has never looked better!

Good-Bye Bottled Water

We used to buy several cases of bottled water each week to drink. Although we always recycled the plastic bottles, we felt guilty contributing so much waste to the landfill. We now probably save about $50 a month on what we were spending on water that was far from healthy to drink in the first place. Yesterday, when I was downtown, it was hot and I was thirsty so I bought a bottle of water to drink. Now that I am used to drinking **God's Miracle Water**™, the bottled water tasted like "Liquid Yuk"! Needless to say, I waited till I got home to quench my thirst.

Improved Memory and Focus

I write self-help books, facilitate workshops, and spend countless hours on the phone counseling clients. I notice that since drinking and bathing in **God's Miracle Water**™, my memory is much sharper, I can focus more easily, and I no longer suffer from low energy around 3:00 in the afternoon. I get more done in 3-4 days than I used to get done in an entire week!

Huge Increase in Energy

For most of my life, I have had enormous resistance to exercising because I never had much energy after working all day. I now have enough energy after working 8-10 hours to easily walk for 1-2 miles. This is a major breakthrough for me. I now look forward to engaging in other forms of exercise to increase my strength, flexibility, and endurance.

No Need for Chlorine in Hot Tub or Pools

We never liked soaking in chlorinated water so we just stopped using our hot tub several years ago. Since we won't have to use much (if any) chlorine or chemicals to keep the water free of bacteria now, we plan to fire up the hot tub again his fall. I look forward to relaxing in a pristine, clean, hot water that hydrates, nourishes, and detoxifies every cell of my body before I go to bed each night.

Wildlife are Wild About God's Miracle Water™

Animals and wildlife love good water too. Since installing **God's Miracle Water System**™, our property has become a sanctuary for more wildlife than ever before. Not only do we see several deer coming to graze and drink from the ponds each day, but the bunny, squirrel, quail, and hummingbird population has increased substantially.

Not only that, but for the first time in 32 years, we have a family of 10 wild turkeys who come to visit us 3-4 times a day. It's like living in a wildlife preserve. We are so-o-o-o blessed.

Thank God for **God's Miracle Water**™.

Being a skeptic by nature and profession, I am a scientist; I am leery of any claims that are put on a product. Show me the proof. When my wife first approached me on a unit that could be attached in line with our water system that would not only improve water but could actually improve our health I could only think she had been suckered in by a fast talking charlatan selling snake oil remedies. I agreed to have a unit (Structured Water) installed on the condition that it came with a money back trial if we were not satisfied. Thinking that this was a no brainier and we would get our money back I could save face and tell my wife "see I told you."

Much to my surprise the first time I took a shower I had the sensation that I had used a conditioner on my head. Truly it could not be that on the very first use that I would feel results. I then decided to drink some and immediately on raising my glass to my mouth realized that it did not smell like our tap water. On tasting the water it was evident that it was different. I am not certain how it works, at least from a scientific point, other than to say that I understood the scientific reason behind the principal. Structured water is an apt name as that is exactly what it does. I am so convinced by the unit that when I asked my wife what was it called she said that the product was so new that they had just recently named it. I told her that it should be called "miracle water". I believe so much in the product that I have purchased additional units for all my family especially for my daughter who has a new born. I would never return this product for any reason.
-- Ed Chacon Archeo Astronomer 2008, Santa Fe, New Mexico

After a long week and a shorter weekend, I was drained on a Sunday. My friend called me and I told him I was really tired of "being tired" all the time. He said he had something for me to try and brought over some water. However, I felt like a new person and so did my wife after she had a couple of glasses. We were both in awe! We had a raw natural energy that we hadn't felt in years! I went from exhausted to feeling 20 years younger, in a matter of an hour!

Now we have a "Structured Water Unit" of our own. The benefits are incredible! We both feel better, our skin is like silk. The "itchy leg syndrome" that seemed to be haunting us and the rest of the country when we try to go to sleep — is gone. That is worth so much in itself, It's hard to stress. The bathtub is clean and does not have the standard mold and buildup associated with showers. We wouldn't go a day without it now . . . I've been drinking "the water". Unreal! My legs have been itching and I scratch them until they bleed. After that bath — no itch. Our hair is soft and — it's a real trip! WOW! We're not sure how the Structured Water Unit does it's magic, but it IS MAGIC! -- Brian Z., Musician – Salt Lake City, Utah

I work at a natural lifestyles company and we have a large vegetable garden that we all work with and eat from. We were forced to replant the vegetable garden after realizing that our plants would not sprout due to large amounts of calcium in our well water system. The calcium had created a hard crust over the soft soil making it impossible for sprouts to penetrate through. When I first heard the simple explanation for how the Structured Water Unit worked I was not expecting much; to be direct, it seemed too simple to be true. In any event, we connected the Garden Unit Structured Water Unit to the hose, and began watering. About this time I left town for 9 days and while I was away we continued to water the garden with the Structured Water Unit. When I returned the garden had not only sprouted, but many of the plants were already 6 inches tall! The garden is now 5 months along and as you can see in the photo's that I sent we have more veggies than we can eat. Also we have noticed that we do not need to water as often as you said, the plants absorb more water because of the lower surface tension of the water after passing through the device. The owners of our company value it so much that they have since installed the Whole House Unit so that they could have structured water for showering and cooking as well. Thank you once again for making this simple and inexpensive product available. -- Michael Copeland, Sacred Health, Sedona,

I'm enjoying drinking my water and showering with your Structured Water Unit. I went 2 days without putting lotion on (which I always do). My skin is definitely more hydrated, but still need lotion to stay looking good by the end of the day. Who knows...... maybe time will change that too. I'll let you know! I'm enjoying drinking my water and showering with your Structured Water Unit. I went 2 days without putting lotion on (which I always do). My skin is definitely more hydrated, just still needs lotion to stay looking good by the end of the day. Who knows...... maybe time will change that too. I'll let you know! Talk with you soon!
-- Deborah, Sedona, AZ

The cats have been drinking the water now for a few days – the youngest one being the first to explore it — she has somewhat of a lazy-eye — I noticed today that it seems to be straightening and she is much more relaxed in her environment and not fighting the condition so much now – awesome sir!!! Many, Many Thanks again!! -- Gene Eskelson, Salt Lake City, Utah

The Structured Water Unit is the most outstanding water alchemist I've ever experienced. My garden has grown twice the size this year that it was the same time last year. Personally, my body has noticed tremendous healing change. I feel more oxygenated in my body. I think this device is outstanding. -- Thea Ivie, ND, Sedona,

Our new 'Structured Water Unit' is producing amazing changes in our water! My skin feels soft and lubricated after bathing. I use less soap and shampoo. Less soap is needed for washing the clothes. The new water has rejuvenated our plants. My husband says our water tastes better too; and morning coffee is smooth – no longer bitter. We love the new I've never been so excited to shower now that we have this unit in our shower. The cats are loving the water already and my skin is feeling great.
-- Missy Norgan, Las Vegas

Drinking only the Structured Water Unit water and eating small amounts of food (raw almonds and yogurt) I was able to work productively for 4 days at a time with only about 3 hours of sleep spread out over this period. During the first week of bathing and drinking the water exclusively, including the 4 day period mentioned before, I started having very powerful synchronistic events almost one after the other. The fabric of the illusion I had been living in began to unravel. After experiencing the water for a couple of months I have improved stamina and better focus, with the ability to change this improved focus very rapidly from one thing to another without hesitation. My ability to get into the zone has improved ten-fold. I practice various styles of internal martial arts and the water has given me a different and more whole experience when practicing. With the water I am learning how to be in the moment in other parts of my life outside of my practice.
-- Stan C. Pagosa Springs, CO

Since I've been using the structured water, I noticed that the water makes my hair softer and my skin too! The Structured Water Unit is a great product. When I drink it I feel refreshed. I like that kind of water. The water we had installed, before we installed The Structured Water Unit, made me hair and face dry and oily, now I feel soft. Well, I got to go. Bye. I am 11 going on 12 years old. -- Allison Krok, Salt Lake City, Utah

Thank you so very much for bringing this extremely important technology to the market place. I am excited to share my reason for writing this letter of thanks. Our vacant lot by the restaurant is growing 15 ft. sunflowers and a lush vegetable garden since using the Structured Water Unit. Kelly Johnson, Bliss Cafe, Sedona, AZ

Chapter 13. Ultimate Destiny Network, Inc.

Income Opportunities Helping Introduce Structured Water

Ultimate Destiny is supporting the work of Clayton Nolte, inventor of Natural Action Structured Water devices. We are seeking intentional communities and retreat centers that would like to enjoy the health, savings, and environmental benefits of "living water," share them with residents/guests, and earn an income when others decide to buy one of the units. There are also opportunities for individuals and communities to earn affiliate commissions helping others learn about these life and energy enhancing products. (See www.ultimatestructuredwater.info/affiliate_program.htm)

This exclusive technology uses an advanced understanding of the vortex phenomenon, utilizing the dynamic characteristic of water itself to create a naturally balanced, "structured water." It alters the molecular structure of the water, activating and retaining the healthful benefits of minerals and characteristics while excess suspended solids, contaminants and sediment are dynamically isolated or removed. Specially tuned geometry creates an energy environment for water to structure itself. This gives water a lower surface tension and better hydrating properties. While both showering and drinking, the geometric configurations break up large, low-energy water molecule clusters into smaller, high-energy clusters. This eliminates negative energy patterns (sometimes called the "memory" of water) and redefines the water's natural healthy energy pattern.

What does that mean to you? This structured water allows the molecules to imprint through the DNA and RNA the knowledge of its secret blueprint and help you to become more balanced in the universe.

We are seeking additional distributors and affiliates to help us introduce our structured water devices. Sign up for the free affiliate program at www.ultimatestructuredwater.info and earn 10% referral commissions.

For the information packet on a distributorship, please contact Charles Betterton at 928-284-2671 or by email at ultimatestructuredwater@gmail.com.

Chapter 14. Ultimate Water for Humanity

Introduction by Charles Betterton, Cofounder of Ultimate Destiny

> **Over one billion people lack safe water, and three billion lack sanitation; eighty per cent of infectious diseases are waterborne, killing millions of children each year. — World Bank Institute, 1999**

Ultimate Water for Humanity is a new non-profit organization to help provide expanded global access to clean water.

> **We are called to be architects of the future, not its victims. The challenge is to make the world work for 100% of humanity in the shortest possible time, with spontaneous cooperation and without ecological damage or disadvantage of anyone. How can we make the world work for 100 percent of humanity in the shortest possible time through spontaneous cooperation without ecological damage or disadvantage to anyone? -- Bucky Fuller**

I have always felt that Bucky Fuller was one of the most brilliant visionaries in recorded history. When some associates and I began co-founding cause-oriented companies and affiliated non-profit organizations a few years ago, our shared vision and mission was (and still is) to help millions of people awaken to who we are, why we are here and what we came to be, do and manifest stewardship over.

One of the web sites where we invite co-creative participation in addressing these questions is at www.creatingyourultimatedestiny.com. We have frequently included quotes by Bucky and have featured resources from the Buckminster Fuller Institute in our printed materials and web sites related to fostering personal, social and planetary empowerment, transformation and sustainability.

A few years ago, Rev. Dr. Audrey Turner, one of the founding board members for what is now Ultimate Destiny Network asked us to consider the following question:

"What would our world be like if none of us could have clean drinking water until all of us do? What about the same question applied to food, shelter, access to opportunities for meaningful employment?"

Over the past few weeks, some of us involved in Ultimate Destiny became acquainted with and have been working with Clayton Nolte, inventor of the Ultimate Structured Water devices. While the significance of the devices is readily apparent from the hundreds of testimonials from all over the world, I felt that it was appropriate to share with our board of directors and investors why I believe the allocation of time and energy to support Clayton's vision is a top priority totally in alignment with our corporate vision and mission. That led to the insights that have resulted in Ultimate Water for Humanity and the web site at **Ultimate Water for Humanity**.

As I brainstormed the various facets that "betterment for 100% of humanity" might entail, I listed the ones that are included as main components of this web site. Each of those draft pages includes a few examples of the types of resources that we will be sharing with others who are interested in any one or more aspects of our vision and mission.

In addition to the resources that are targeted to a specific area of focus, here a few examples of other more general resources we will provide access to as featured resources: All of these initial resources have been developed by the cause-oriented company Ultimate Destiny Network as components of the 14-part, 1,200+ page Ultimate Destiny Success System that is available from the affiliated NPO, Ultimate Destiny University.

Manifesting Your Ultimate Destiny
Solving Your Ultimate Destiny Success Puzzle
Fostering Personal and Planetary Sustainability
Solving Our Personal, Community and Global Success Puzzles

We will also be providing access to resources on co-creative visioning and strategic planning, publishing, electronic publishing and Internet marketing, establishing strategic alliances and applying "Strategic Marketing Systems".

Charles Betterton, MSCED (Community Economic Development)

Chapter 15. Featured Educational Resources

More Articles about Structured Water

New Structured Water Devices Hydrate the Body

Article written by Renee Trenda

Inventor, Clayton Nolte, has unveiled new water devices that offer excellent hydration and detoxification properties for the body. He calls his products Ultimate Structured Water Devices.

Nolte says that his devices are based on how nature purifies water in the oceans and rivers. He has observed that nature uses a process of dynamic motion of all kinds, tumbling the water every which way and making it run through vortices in order to restructure the water and make it pure again.

So Nolte's devices do the same thing. His Ultimate Structured Water Devices have geometrically shaped chambers inside of the unit That cause the water to swirl in a vortex fashion, sort of like a tornado, both clock-wise and counter clock-wise at the same time. Next, the water passes through a field of glass beads that causes the water to tumble every which way, adding even more motion and momentum in the process.

When regular unstructured tap water flows into the inlet side of the device, the water that comes out the other end is both soft and structured, after going through the natural cleansing process that happens within the unit.

There are many benefits to using the structured water.

* Has a very small water molecule that can easily absorb toxins.

* PH is balanced

* Is soft due to the purifying effect and lack of pollutants in the water

* Has no "Memory"

* Has high life force energy

The structured water has a natural intelligence that allows it to discern what is good for the body and what is harmful for it. It absorbs the things that are bad for the body, like chlorine and fluoride, and holds them in isolation for safe removal from the body. And if there is still room in the water molecule, it will start pulling other toxins such as viruses, bacteria, pesticides and other harmful chemicals from your body as well. In other words, this natural water will detoxify your body.

The second huge benefit that this unit delivers, is that it really helps to hydrate the cells of the body and that includes all the organs, tissues, and skin, and helps to balance the PH of the fluids of the body. That amounts to anti-aging, and boosting the immune system. All from drinking the right kind of water.

Clayton Nolte has developed several different size units for home, garden and commercial use. There are testimonials on the website from customers all over the world regarding the water in livestock operations, greenhouse applications and public restaurants as well as home and personal use.

A New Structured Water Purification Device is Unveiled

Article written by Renee Trenda

People are giving rave reviews to a brand new water device brought out by inventor Clayton Nolte. He calls his product the Ultimate Structured Water Device. Truthfully, it is quite unique in that it has no moving parts, no filter, does not depend on electricity or magnetics, and it will never wear out. In fact Clayton offers a lifetime replacement guarantee. Those features alone give it top marks for sustainability.

Nolte has studied water for decades and has based the design of his devices on how he perceives that Mother Earth cleans and energizes water in nature. His inventions mimic the activity found in a rapidly running river.

Here's how it works:

The Ultimate Water Devices have geometrically shaped chambers inside of the unit that cause the water to swirl in a vortex fashion, sort of like a tornado, both clock-wise and counter clock-wise at the same time. Next, the water passes through a field of glass beads that causes the water to tumble every which way, adding even more motion and momentum in the process.

Regular unstructured tap water goes in the inlet side of the device, and the water that comes out the other end is both soft and structured, after going through the natural cleansing process that is achieved as a result of the dynamic tumbling motion within the unit.

Nolte says there is quite a bit of difference between unstructured water and structured water.

Unstructured Tap Water:

* Has a large clustered molecule that is too big to hydrate cells

* PH varies according to the pollutants in the water

* Can be "Hard" due to the pollutants in the water

* Retains the "Memory" and condition of where it has been

* Has little life force energy

Structured Water:

* Has a very small water molecule that can easily absorb toxins and detoxify the body.

* PH is balanced

* Is soft due to the purifying effect and lack of pollutants in the water

* Has no "Memory"

* Has high life force energy

Nolte has observed that structured water has a natural intelligence that allows it to discern what is good for life and what is harmful for life. It assimilates the things that are bad for life and carries them away. For example, chlorine, fluoride and other toxins are bad for life, so the structured water takes them into its cells for disposal. What you will consume in the water from this small machine, is the water with the toxins locked inside of it where they are unable to harm your body as they pass through. And if there is still room in the water molecule, it will start pulling other toxins such as viruses, bacteria, pesticides and other harmful chemicals from your body. In other words, the structured water will detoxify your body.

Distilled water and RO water do not have the same natural intelligence that structured water does. We became accustomed to drinking distilled and RO water because they are free of chemicals. However, they are also Dead Waters in the sense that they have very little life force due to the processing methods that were used to create them. They are so empty inside, that they absorb as waste the very elements that natural water tries to deliver as nutrients.

Clayton Nolte has definitely come up with something different here. He is amassing some very passionate testimonials from people who are praising what this device is doing for them in many different ways.

Structuring Makes Water Even Wetter

Article Written by Kimberley Jace

The water found in nature is almost always in motion – either running down a river, crashing to the shore in waves, being moved by wind and currents, or evaporating and condensing. Non-moving water molecules tend to "cluster," forming weak electromagnetic bonds with other water molecules and also bonding with any pollutants in the water.

The tumbling action of moving water tends to break water molecules into smaller, highly-energized clusters and break the bonds between water molecules and pollutants. Water in small clusters, without bonds to any solubles, is called "structured water."

Structured water is more easily assimilated into the body because it has lower surface tension and the smaller molecule clusters can pass more easily through membranes, which aids in hydration. The human body is more than 70 percent water; the water locked within human body cells at birth is structured water.

During the aging process, that water supply decreases; structured water can help replace intra-cellular water, thereby slowing the aging process. Structured water also enables the body to rid itself of toxins more easily.

The Essenes, a Jewish religious group who lived around the time of Christ, were said to have made water pitchers with structures in the spouts that tumbled the water as it poured out. Water structuring devices are sold today that tumble and spin the water as it comes out of the shower or kitchen sink faucet.

Whole-house systems are available that structure the water at intervals so that every home faucet delivers structured water. Some spas, including the Angel Valley Resort in Sedona, Ariz., use structured water for everything: cooking, cleaning, drinking, showering, and landscaping.

Users who shower or bathe in structured water say their hair and skin stays hydrated longer. There is anecdotal evidence showing benefits to animals and plants given structured water. Most things that require water require less structured water because of its superior hydrating ability.

Because the water molecules are not electromagnetically bound to any pollutants that may be present, structured water is better at washing away toxins and helping the body eliminate them.

Structuring also is thought to have a quantum effect on water. Water carries emotional "memories" of everything is encounters. The structuring process cleanses water of memory and emotion, allowing it to hydrate without carrying this subtle energy pollution. Some say water can be structured through intention alone: focusing mental energy on water will break the weak electromagnetic bonds that form water molecule clusters.

Another quantum effect of structured water is that it tends to structure other water in its vicinity. Some U.S. water dowsers systematically cleanse and energize standing bodies of water throughout the country by adding small amounts of structured water.

Water Facts-- From Life Experience - Why Water Matters!

(Reprinted with permission from Experience Life www.experiencelife.com)

Even healthy eaters often underestimate the importance of their water intake and wind up suffering from chronic, low-grade dehydration. Here are just a few reasons good hydration is essential to good health, followed by six tips for staying hydrated:

Energy: Suboptimal hydration slows the activity of enzymes, including those responsible for producing energy, leading to feelings of fatigue. Even a slight reduction in hydration can lower metabolism and reduce your ability to exercise efficiently.

Digestion: Our bodies produce an average of 7 liters of digestive juices daily. When we don't drink enough liquid, our secretions are more limited and the digestive process is inhibited. (Note that drinking too much water all at once, particularly with food, can also dilute digestive juices, reducing their efficacy and leading to indigestion.)

Regularity: As partially digested food passes through the colon, the colon absorbs excess liquid and transfers it to the bloodstream so that a stool of normal consistency is formed. When the body is low on water, it extracts too much liquid from the stool, which then becomes hard, dry and difficult to eliminate. Slowed elimination contributes to bodywide toxicity and inflammation.

Blood Pressure: When we are chronically dehydrated, our blood becomes thicker and more viscous. Additionally, in response to reduced overall blood volume, the blood vessels contract. To compensate for the increased vein-wall tension and increased blood viscosity, the body must work harder to push blood through the veins, resulting in elevated blood pressure.

Stomach Health: Under normal circumstances, the stomach secretes a layer of mucus (which is composed of 98 percent water) to prevent its mucus membranes from being destroyed by the highly acidic digestive fluid it produces. Chronic dehydration, though, impedes mucus production and may irritate and produce ulcers in the stomach lining.

Respiration: The moist mucus membranes in the respiratory region are protective; however, in a state of chronic dehydration, they dry out and become vulnerable to attack from substances that might exist in inhaled air, such as dust and pollen.

Acid-Alkaline Balance: Dehydration causes enzymatic slowdown, interrupting important biochemical transformations, with acidifying results at the cellular level. The acidification of the body's internal cellular environment can be further worsened when excretory organs responsible for eliminating acids (e.g., the skin and kidneys) don't have enough liquid to do their jobs properly. An overly acidic biochemical environment can give rise to a host of inflammatory health conditions, as well as yeast and fungus growth.

Weight Management: Feelings of thirst can be confused with hunger, both because eating can soothe thirst and also because dehydration-induced fatigue is often misinterpreted as a lack of fuel (e.g., sugar). Both dynamics can lead to false sensations of hunger, triggering overeating and weight gain. Inadequate hydration can also promote the storage of inflammatory toxins, which can also promote weight gain.

Skin Health: Dehydrated skin loses elasticity and has a dry, flaky appearance and texture. But dehydration can also lead to skin irritation and rashes, including conditions like eczema. We need to sweat about 24 ounces a day to properly dilute and transport the toxins being eliminated through our skin. When we are chronically dehydrated, the sweat becomes more concentrated and toxins aren't removed from our systems as readily, which can lead to skin irritation and inflammation.

Cholesterol: Cholesterol is an essential element in cell membrane construction. When we are in a state of chronic dehydration and too much liquid is removed from within the cell walls, the body tries to stop the loss by producing more cholesterol to shore up the cell membrane. Although the cholesterol protects the cell membrane from being so permeable, the overproduction introduces too much cholesterol into the bloodstream.

Kidney and Urinary Health: When we don't drink enough liquid, our kidneys struggle to flush water-soluble toxins from our system. When we don't adequately dilute the toxins in our urine, the toxins irritate the urinary mucus membranes and create a germ- and infection-friendly environment.

Joint Health: Dehydrated cartilage and ligaments are more brittle and prone to damage. Joints can also become painfully inflamed when irritants, usually toxins produced by the body and concentrated in our blood and cellular fluids, attack them, setting the stage for arthritis.

Aging: The normal aging process involves a gradual loss of cell volume and an imbalance of the extracellular and intracellular fluids. This loss of cellular water can be accelerated when we don't ingest enough liquids, or when our cell membranes aren't capable of maintaining a proper fluid balance.

6 Tips for Staying Hydrated

1. Start each day with a glass of water (no ice). Drink it down before you have coffee, tea or juice. It will help replace fluids lost overnight and get your hydration efforts off to a good start. Also fill a water bottle you can take with you in the car, or keep with you and refill during the workday.

2. Eat two or three servings of fruits and vegetables at every meal. They are brimming with water and include the minerals that help your body absorb and use it properly. Keep in mind that most processed foods (including sugars, flours, salty snacks and processed meats) result in a lowering of the body's water table. Eating a lot of meat puts pressure on your kidneys and tends to increase your body's need for water.

3. Establish regular water breaks, if possible. Tailor your drinking to meet your needs. For instance, drink an extra glass of water if you worked out or didn't squeeze enough fruits and vegetables into your day.

4. Substitute sparkling water and low-sodium vegetable juice for soda and fruit juice. While it's true that all beverages count toward your daily tally, the sugar in regular soda and fruit juice, as well as the chemicals in diet versions, can trigger a host of unwanted reactions in the body, including blood-sugar spikes.

5. Install a Structured Water unit in your home and use a portable unit at the office. Resort to bottled water when you must, but beware of the drawbacks: It's expensive and environmentally wasteful, the plastic

contains harmful chemicals that can leach into the water, and there are no guarantees that bottled water is any better for you than the water flowing from the tap.

6. Cook with high-quality sea salt. A good, unrefined sea salt is rich in trace minerals, which are key to cell health and hydration. Bonus: Sea salt is also lower in sodium than table salt.

Eight Myths about Dehydration

Myth No. 1: Dehydration is relatively rare and occurs only when the body is deprived of water for days.

Reality: Low-grade dehydration (versus acute and clinical dehydration) is a chronic, widespread problem that has major impacts on well-being, energy, appearance and resiliency. Christopher Vasey, ND, a Swiss naturopath and author of The Water Prescription (Healing Arts Press, 2006), believes that most people suffer regularly from this type of chronic dehydration because of poor eating and drinking habits.

Chronic dehydration can cause digestive disorders because our bodies need water to produce the digestive juices that aid the digestive process. If we don't get that water, we don't secrete enough digestive juices, and a variety of problems – such as gas, bloating, nausea, poor digestion and loss of appetite – can ensue.

Bottom Line: If you're not actively focusing on hydrating throughout the day, there's a good chance you could be at least somewhat dehydrated, which could be negatively affecting your energy, vitality and immunity – as well as your appearance. Experiment with drinking more water throughout the day. You may observe an almost immediate difference in your well-being, and even if you don't, establishing good hydration habits now will do many good things for your cellular health over the long haul.

Myth No. 2: Your body needs eight, 8-ounce glasses of water daily.

Reality: Your body does need a steady supply of water to operate efficiently and perform the many routine housekeeping tasks that keep you healthy and energetic.

That said, there is no scientific evidence to back up the very specific and well-worn advice that you need to drink eight, 8-ounce glasses of water a day (a.k.a. the 8 x 8 rule). In 2002, Heinz Valtin, MD, a retired physiology professor from Dartmouth Medical School and author of two textbooks on kidney function, published the definitive paper on the subject in the American Journal of Physiology. He spent 10 months searching medical literature for scientific evidence of the 8 x 8 rule only to come up empty-handed.

In 2004, the Institute of Medicine (IOM), a division of the National Academy of Sciences, actually set the adequate total-daily-water intake at higher than 64 ounces – 3.7 liters (125 fluid ounces) for men and 2.7 liters (91 fluid ounces) for women. But those numbers refer to total water intake, meaning all beverages and water-containing foods count toward your daily quota. Fruits and veggies, for example, pack the most watery punch, with watermelon and cucumbers topping the list.

But the "it all counts" dynamic cuts both ways. Vasey believes that many people suffer from low-grade, chronic dehydration because of what they are eating as well as what they are drinking. The "I don't like water" crowd could probably make up their water deficits by eating the right kinds of foods, he asserts, "but most don't eat enough fruits and vegetables. Instead they eat meat, cereals and breads, which don't have much water and contain a lot of salt."

Animal proteins require a great deal more moisture than they contain to break down, assimilate and then flush from the body. And many processed foods, such as chips and crackers, for example, are nearly devoid of moisture, so – like dry sponges – they soak up water as they proceed through the digestive system.

The body requires only 3 to 5 grams of salt a day to stay healthy, but most people gobble up 12 to 15 grams of the stuff daily. To rid itself of the overload, the body requires copious amounts of liquid.

Bottom Line: If you want to stay optimally healthy, hydrated and energetic, it's a good idea to eat plenty of water-containing foods and drink water throughout the day. And when in doubt, it's probably not a bad idea to make a point of drinking a little more water, rather than a little less. But that doesn't mean you need to down eight glasses exactly, or that if you run a little shy of 64 ounces, then something awful is going to happen.

Just be aware that the fewer vegetables, fruits and legumes you are eating, and the more dried, processed or chemical-laced foods you include in your diet, the more water you'll need to consume to compensate.

Myth No. 3: When it comes to hydrating, all beverages are created equal.

Reality: Not so. In principle, the 90 to 125 (or so) ounces recommended by the Institute of Medicine would include your morning coffee, the soda you drink with lunch and even a glass of wine at dinner. Practically speaking, however, caffeinated, sweetened and alcoholic drinks pack chemical cargoes (or trigger chemical reactions) that demand significant amounts of fluid to properly process and filter. As a result, nonwater beverages can actually set you back, water-wise, many experts suggest. "They can actually dehydrate the body," says Haas.

For example, says Vasey, drinks like coffee, black tea and cocoa are very high in purines, toxins that must be diluted in large quantities of water to be flushed from the body.

Artificially sweetened drinks add to the body's toxic burden. Sugar and coffee also create an acidic environment in the body, impeding enzyme function and taxing the kidneys, which must rid the body of excess acid.

Moreover, says Vasey, caffeine found in coffee, black tea and soft drinks adversely affects your body's water stores because it is a diuretic that elevates blood pressure, increasing the rate of both the production and elimination of urine.

"The water in these drinks travels through the body too quickly," says Vasey. "Hardly has the water entered the bloodstream than the kidneys remove a portion of the liquid and eliminate it, before the water has time to make its way into the intracellular environment." (For more on the importance of intracellular hydration, see "Myth No. 5.")

Bottom Line: Moderate consumption of beverages like coffee and tea is fine, but be aware that while some of the fluids in nonwater beverages may be helping you, certain ingredients may be siphoning away your body's water stores. So, when you're drinking to hydrate, stick primarily with water. And, if you're looking for a pick-me-up, try sparkling water with a squeeze of citrus.

Myth No. 4: By the time you get thirsty, you're already dehydrated.

Reality: Again, it depends on what you mean by "dehydrated." Experts like Vasey posit that while those walking around in a state of subclinical dehydration may not feel thirst, their bodies are sending other signals of inadequate hydration – from headaches and stomachaches to low energy to dry skin.

But when it comes to avoiding the more widely accepted definition of clinical dehydration, thirst is a good indicator of when you need to swig. Here's the deal: As water levels in the body drop, the blood gets thicker. When the concentration of solids in the blood rises by 2 percent, the thirst mechanism is triggered. A 1 percent rise in blood solids could be called "mild dehydration," but it could also be considered a normal fluctuation in bodily fluids.

Either way, feeling thirsty is a good indicator that you need to get some water into your body, and soon. Serious symptoms of dehydration don't arise until blood solids rise by 5 percent – long after you feel thirsty. But, obviously, you don't want to wait that long. Even mild, subclinical levels of dehydration come with sacrifices in optimal vitality, metabolism and appearance. Like an underwatered plant, the body can survive on less water than it wants, but it's unlikely to thrive.

Bottom Line: Drinking water only when you're thirsty may relegate you to being less than optimally hydrated much of the time, and it may undermine your energy and vitality. On the other hand, constantly sipping or gulping calorie- or chemical-laden beverages for entertainment is a bad idea. So if you tend to keep a bottle of soda on your desk all day, or if you're never seen without your coffee cup in hand, rethink your approach. Get in the habit of drinking a glass of water first thing in the morning, and a few more glasses of water throughout the day. Also drink proactively (especially important during strenuous exercise, long airplane flights and in hot weather).

Myth No. 5: Hydrating is all about water.

Reality: Nope. It takes a delicate balance of minerals, electrolytes and essential fatty acids to get and keep water where it needs to be – properly hydrating your bloodstream, your tissues and your cells.

"You can drink lots of water and still be dehydrated on a cellular level," says Haas. Water you drink is absorbed from the digestive tract into the bloodstream by small blood vessels (capillaries). Of the water contained in food and beverages, 95 percent ends up in the blood. From the blood, water moves into the fluid surrounding the cells, called extracellular fluid. That's important, but it's not the end of the line. Water needs to get inside cells for you to maintain optimal health.

A person's vitality is affected by how well his or her body gets water into and out of cells, says Haas. A variety of unhealthy lifestyle habits and health conditions can inhibit this cellular capacity, he notes. But naturally, too, as the body ages, the water inside cells (intracellular) tends to diminish, and water outside cells (extracellular or interstitial fluid) tends to accumulate. Haas calls this gradual drying out of cells a "biomarker of aging."

Minerals, especially electrolytes and trace minerals, are essential to maintaining cellular equilibrium. Minerals help transport water into the cells, where they also activate enzymes. And enzymes are the basis of every biological process in the body, from digestion to hormone secretion to cognition. Without minerals, says Haas, enzymes get sluggish and the body suffers.

Without essential fatty acids – which form the basis for cellular membranes – cells can't properly absorb, hold and stabilize the water and other nutrients they're supposed to contain.

Bottom Line: Take in plenty of minerals by eating lots of fresh fruits, vegetables, nuts and seeds – ideally from produce grown according to biodynamic farming practices, meaning the farmer is supporting (rather than depleting) nutrients in the soil. Another way to boost minerals in the diet is cooking with a high-quality sea salt. A natural, unrefined sea salt will deliver up to 60 trace minerals your body needs to manage water flow.

Also, try to include whole foods that are high in essential fatty acids, such as walnuts and flax seeds, which are critical to maintaining healthy cell membranes that can hold in moisture. And consider a multimineral supplement that includes an ample supply of trace minerals in its formulation.

Myth No. 6: Healthy urine is always clear.

Reality: Urine color is directly linked to hydration status because the yellow tint is a measure of how many solid particles, such as sodium, chloride, nitrogen and potassium, are excreted. The color's intensity depends on how much water the kidneys mix with the solids. Less water equals darker urine. More water equals lighter urine. Dark or rank-smelling urine are signs your body may need more water. But light-to-medium yellow urine is fine. Very clear urine may actually be a signal that your kidneys are taxed by the amount of fluid moving through them and the minerals in your body are being too diluted.

Also note that some vitamins, such as riboflavin, or B2, can turn urine bright yellow, so don't be alarmed if your urine is a funny color after either swallowing a multivitamin or eating certain foods, like nutritional yeast, which is high in B vitamins.

Bottom Line: Drink enough water to make light yellow (lemonade-colored) urine. The volume depends on your activity level and metabolism. If your urine is cloudy or dark or foul smelling, increase your water intake and monitor changes. If you don't see a positive change, consult a health professional.

Myth No. 7: Drinking too much water leads to water retention.

Reality: The body retains water in response to biochemical and hormonal imbalances, toxicity, poor cardiovascular and cellular health – and, interestingly, dehydration. "If you're not drinking enough liquid, your body may actually retain water to compensate," says Vasey, adding that a general lack of energy is the most common symptom of this type of water retention. "Paradoxically, you can sometimes eliminate fluid retention by drinking more water, not less, because if you ingest enough water, the kidneys do not try and retain water by cutting back on elimination," he explains.

Bottom Line: No good comes of drinking less water than you need. If you have water-retention problems, seek professional counsel to help you identify the root cause (food intolerances, for example, are a common culprit in otherwise healthy people). Do not depend on diuretics or water avoidance to solve your problems, since both strategies will tend to make the underlying healthy challenges worse, not better.

Myth No. 8: You can't drink too much water.

Reality: Under normal conditions, the body flushes the water it doesn't need. But it is possible – generally under extreme conditions when you are drinking more than 12 liters in 24 hours or exercising heavily – to disrupt the body's osmotic balance by diluting and flushing too much sodium, an electrolyte that helps balance the pressure of fluids inside and outside of cells. That means cells bloat from the influx and may even burst.

While the condition, called hyponatremia, is rare, it happens. Long-distance runners are at highest risk for acute hyponatremia (meaning the imbalance happens in less than 48 hours), but anyone can get in trouble if they drink water to excess without replacing essential electrolytes and minerals. Extreme overconsumption of water can also strain the kidneys and, if drunk with meals, interfere with proper digestion.

Chronic hyponatremia, meaning sodium levels gradually taper off over days or weeks, is less dangerous because the brain can gradually adjust to the deficit, but the condition should still be treated by a doctor. Chronic hyponatremia is often seen in adults with illnesses that leach sodium from the body, such as kidney disease and congestive heart failure. But even a bad case of diarrhea, especially in children, can set the stage for hyponatremia. Be on the lookout for symptoms such as headache, confusion, lethargy and appetite loss.

Bottom Line: Never force yourself to drink past a feeling of fullness. If you are drinking copious amounts of water and still experiencing frequent thirst, seek help from a health professional. If you're drinking lots of fluids to fuel an exercise regimen that lasts longer than one hour, be sure to accompany your water with adequate salts and electrolytes. For information on wise fitness-hydration strategies, read "How to Hydrate" in our December 2007 archives at experiencelifemag.com.

Vasey hopes that health-motivated people will return to the simple pleasures of water in much the same way they've recently rediscovered the myriad benefits of whole foods over heavily processed and aggressively marketed industrial fare. "Nature gave us water, not soft drinks," he says. "It's time to get back to basics."

Fostering Personal and Planetary Sustainability from Ultimate Destiny.

Fostering Personal and Planetary Sustainability

What kind of world are we leaving for those who come after us? What kind of life are we creating for ourselves, right now?

The life we lead, the talents we have been given, and the material possessions we enjoy all factor into our stewardship for both the world and our personal lives.

Fostering Personal and Planetary Sustainability will start you moving in the direction of re-inventing your way of living on the planet. You will get a clear picture of where your thoughts and actions are sustainable and healthy, and where you may want to make changes.

You will develop a workable plan to enjoyably cooperate with nature and gain the satisfaction of both thinking about sustainability and acting on it as well. This digital program will show you how to create the vision of a life lived responsibly and then set the goals, develop action plans, and assemble the teams of likeminded people to help create a better world.

Fostering Personal and Planetary Sustainability will help you find real sustainability. Develop a healthy recognition of local and global resources. Taking good care of yourself and your planet will become an automatic and joyful part of your life.

Fostering Personal and Planetary Sustainability is one of 14 interactive programs contained within the ***Ultimate Destiny Success System*** from Ultimate Destiny University. It includes self-assessment quizzes, featured resources, and other tools for taking the first steps toward sustainability.

To discover more ways to foster conscious and sustainable living, please visit
http://www.fosteringpersonalandplanetarysustainability.com

To receive your copy of the E-book on a donation basis with the proceeds being donated to Ultimate Water for Humanity, please send an email with the words "Sustainability E-book" in the subject line to ultimatedestinynetwork@gmail.com

Seven Keys for Personal and Planetary Transformation

Excerpted with Permission from *Rediscover Your Heart: 7 Keys for Personal and Planetary Transformation* by Fred Matser

Key 1: We can trust in the guiding hand of the Divine. Affirmation: I trust that everything has a divine purpose from which it is possible to learn and grow.

Key 2: We can free our minds to explore new horizons. Affirmation: I can go beyond my conventional belief systems and open up to infinite possibilities.

Key 3: We can rediscover our hearts and serve humanity. Affirmation: By expanding my consciousness I can integrate my mind and heart and serve humanity compassionately.

Key 4: We can empower ourselves. Affirmation: I choose to free myself from fear to allow changes within and without. In supporting myself and others in this process we can together develop a caring and sharing society.

Key 5: We can live in the spirit of unity. Affirmation: By learning to integrate different parts of my being and focusing on our common humanity I can work for the interests of all.

Key 6: We can find our own path to truth. Affirmation: May I have the courage to explore the mysteries of life and seek the truth without judgment.

Key 7: We can make a difference. Affirmation: My personal development is linked to global transformation and I am aware that each one of us counts. I honor the global family of which I am part and cherish the home planet that we all share.

Fred Matser, humanitarian and philanthropist and author of ***Rediscover Your Heart: 7 Keys for Personal and Planetary Transformation*** (2009, Findhorn Press) has launched the Rediscover Your Heart Awards to support young people in direct, inspirational action for personal and global change.

http://www.rediscoveryourheart.org/about.html